Praise

'*Piggy Bank to Portfolio* fills a huge lacuna – something that was clearly missing in addressing financial literacy. Often, parents are reluctant or miss the opportunity to talk to their children about financial education. This easy-to-read book will go a long way in aiding our future generation appreciate the value of money, understand the benefits of savings and make sound investment decisions. I highly recommend this book to every parent. As it is rightly said – an investment in knowledge pays the best interest.'
– **Deepak Parekh, Chairman, HDFC Ltd**

'As a parent to young children I hope to impart to them wisdom about the role of money in life as well as the importance of managing their finances properly. This book provides a great recipe on how to raise financially literate and responsible kids.'
– **Kunal Bahl, Co-founder & CEO, Snapdeal**

'The pandemic has made us revisit our mental and physical practices. But an often overlooked aspect that is as crucial is financial literacy. Families provide the first classroom for their children, and financial literacy must be an integral part of that curriculum.

There is a plethora of free tools and resources from Investopedia to Varsity. While these tools are indispensable for adults, the technique to teach children is most effective when practical. For example, when teaching budgeting, instead of presenting theory through excel sheets, a simple practical example such as providing a child an allowance and asking them to manage it for their expenses like ice-creams or bus fares not only boosts their self-esteem but also encourages them to become curious at an early age on educating themselves.

Binal and Soneera's initiative to inculcate these habits early is crucial now more than ever. We must collectively create a culture where financial literacy is embedded as a priority.'
– **Nikhil Kamath, Co-founder, True Beacon and Zerodha**

'An excellent book to teach your child financial responsibility.'
– **Rakesh Jhunjhunwala, Founder, Rare Enterprises**

'Today a kid finds all her answers online. But it is the parents who need to help them tackle the biggest puzzle of all, finance. Once a child understands the value of a piggy bank and expands it to a portfolio, India will be a strong nation. *Piggy Bank to Portfolio* is a must for every parent. It is a beautifully written, easy-to-understand book that will help parents talk about money to their kid. It might teach them a few things too!'
– **Vijay Shekhar Sharma, CEO, Paytm**

'This book is bursting with practical ways to incorporate money lessons into your child's upbringing. Binal and Soneera's easy-to-read, conversational style will have you thinking about your own money values and help you raise financially confident and compassionate kids.'
– **Zarin Daruwala, CEO, Standard Chartered Bank, India**

Piggy Bank to Portfolio

Piggy Bank to Portfolio

How to Raise Financially Smart Kids

Binal Gandhi and Soneera Sanghvi

JUGGERNAUT BOOKS
C-I-128, First Floor, Sangam Vihar, Near Holi Chowk,
New Delhi 110080, India

First published by Juggernaut Books 2021

Copyright © Binal Gandhi and Soneera Sanghvi 2021

10 9 8 7 6 5 4 3

P-ISBN: 9789391165390
E-ISBN: 9789391165406

All rights reserved. No part of this publication may be reproduced, transmitted, or stored in a retrieval system in any form or by any means without the written permission of the publisher.

Typeset in Adobe Caslon Pro by R. Ajith Kumar, New Delhi

Printed at Thomson Press India Ltd

Dedicated to our children
Annika & Ansh
Mira & Riya

Contents

1. Why Talk to Kids About Money — 1
2. Pocket Money or Not — 17
3. Of Piggy and Other Banks — 45
4. Shopping Trips and More! — 61
5. Grow Your Own Money Tree! — 87
6. Conscious Borrowing — 115
7. Thanking our Stars – Gratitude and Giving — 131
8. To Be or Not To Be – Making a Career Choice — 143

Notes — 164
Select Bibliography — 169
Acknowledgements — 174
A Note on the Authors — 178

1

Why Talk to Kids About Money

Mom: 'What do you think I am, made of money?'
Child: 'Isn't that what MOM stands for?'

- Can you buy me a new game/Lego set/doll house?
- Why do you work? Why can't you spend more time with me?
- Why can't we go for an international vacation?
- Why is that man poor? Are we rich?
- Why can't I have a new smartphone? All my friends have one!
- Can I take my friends to (insert really expensive place) for my birthday?
- Where does the money we put in the bank go?
- Why do we have to wait to buy a new car?

Do these questions sound familiar? If you are like the many parents we interviewed for this book, your child must've asked you at least one of these questions. Money is not an easy topic to discuss. When we raise our kids, we focus on good manners, values, education and exposure, but we often avoid talking to kids about the basics of money – how we earn it, spend it, save it, invest it and, most importantly, how we value it.

Parents put off talking to children about money for various reasons. Some worry that their children are too small. As a parent put it, 'They have to grow up and deal with that anyway, why ruin their childhood now?' Some think that talking to children about money will make them money-minded. Other parents don't know what to tell their kids about money.

Our survey of over 500 parents shows that 41 per cent feel that they do not know enough about money themselves or they do not know what to teach their kids about money. Another 31 per cent feel that the kids could learn about money on their own when they grow older.

The reality is that money-related habits in children start forming at an early age – by age 7, as shown in a Cambridge study.[1] And parents are the biggest influencers when it comes to good money habits in their children. So, if you have any doubts on when to start talking to children about money the answer is now. If your children are older and you haven't started discussing money, it's never too late to start.

'Sometimes parents wait until their kids are in their teens before they start talking about managing money – when they could be starting when their kids are in preschool,' says billionaire investor Warren Buffett. In fact, he says, the biggest mistake parents make when teaching kids about money is that they start too late.[2]

As parents, we do not want our children to make the same mistakes we did – be it saving too late, investing too little or borrowing too much or even paying interest and late fees. Our survey for this book shows that 62 per cent of parents wish they had learned more about money when they were younger.

Your child's attitude and money habits when they become adults will play a large role in their life. Their ability to make sound financial decisions will give them the freedom to choose what they want to do with their lives, which is the key to happiness.

Financial education isn't about teaching kids financial theories every day and giving them homework. It is about being a good role model, talking to them about some of the money-related decisions you make and giving them enough opportunities to gain practical experience with money. Conversations with children about money are opportunities to help them understand and develop healthy financial habits. It's a chance to help them understand your family values and views about money.

Teaching children about money is tricky because money means different things to different people. One's luxury may be another's necessity and a third's frivolity. Some parents equate money with security, some with luxuries, some with hard work and a few even view it as a necessary evil. Our survey reveals the disparity in parents' feelings towards money (see figure on the next page).

So how do you talk to your child about money and how do you teach children the value of money? These are the questions we tackle in this book. We wrote this book with one aim – to help you raise financially prudent children who

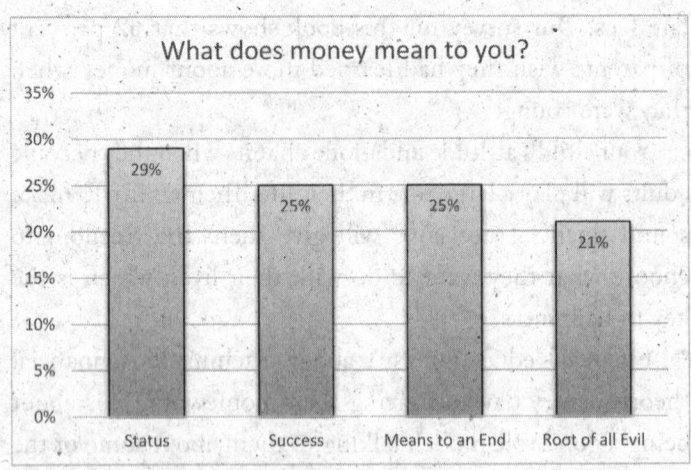

Source: Piggy Bank to Portfolio Parents' Survey

are comfortable handling money. Every chapter includes age-appropriate activities and worksheets for children under 12. For teenagers (because they're not going to sit and do worksheets with you!), we have small tasks built into everyday routines. These tasks will help them gain hands-on experience with money and make learning fun and practical. The Money Talks section, at the end of every chapter, answers commonly asked questions that parents can use as conversation starters when discussing money with their children. Think of this as our curation of Financial FAQs.

Your children will grow up (too quickly) and spend your money (even quicker), they will earn their own money, decide what career path to take, and eventually start saving for their own future. Whether we like it or not, all aspects of our lives have something to do with money. And whether we have a lot or a little, core financial values don't (and shouldn't) change with financial means and status.

We discuss these core values in-depth in each chapter.

There is no money tree

Money, for 99 per cent of us, is a finite resource. We work hard, make sacrifices, and take risks so we can have enough money for our needs and wants. Chapter 2 discusses the pros and cons of pocket money and the importance of self-control and budgeting.

Spending–Saving = Yin–Yang

Spending and saving are best done when balanced with each other. Spending is about happiness now and saving is about happiness in the future. Chapters 3 and 4 give you tools to help your children balance this see-saw.

Money doesn't equal love, happiness or self-worth

Money cannot buy happiness. Research shows that after a certain income level, more money does not make a significant difference in a person's life satisfaction.[3] Children must learn that a fancy brand or car is not what defines them, or their self-worth. Chapter 4 addresses peer pressure and discusses how to instil good spending habits from a young age.

Creating wealth

Rs 10 lakh saved today when your child is 5 years old will not be worth the same when your child is 20 and wants to do an expensive postgraduation course. Chapter 5 discusses the significance of inflation, passive income, and the importance of investing early. Our anecdotes and tips will help you encourage budding Jhunjhunwalas and Buffetts.

Living within our means

When we grew up, our comparisons were restricted to our social circle, not social media. Lifestyle upgrades and consumerism have changed the way Indians look at borrowing. Chapter 6 discusses how to teach our children the cost and consequences of borrowing.

Giving back

As incomes grow, parents are concerned about raising entitled children. Chapter 7 discusses how to instil the practice of gratitude and the importance of giving from a young age.

Planning for the future

'What do you want to be when you grow up?' Chapter 8 discusses how to help our children explore different career paths and choose a career that is fulfilling emotionally and financially.

Our children will have a healthy, productive relationship with money if they can master these values. As parents, we can give our children all the financial wisdom in the world but it will mean nothing if we don't practise what we preach. So before you embark on this financial journey with your child(ren), be mindful of the following:

Be a good role model

Kids learn by watching you, your behaviour and how you deal with money. If you're a compulsive shopper don't expect your child to be thrifty. If mom or dad routinely go over budget, the children will think – why budget?

Be consistent

Before you talk to your children about money, your partner and you must be on the same page (easier said than done, we know). The quiz at the end of this chapter is a good starting point for your partner and you to discover your financial values and how to approach your child's financial education. Consistency will ensure that the financial lessons you want to teach are not lost.

Show sensitivity and patience

Your children will make mistakes. That is the whole point of starting early. Allow your children to make these mistakes and let them learn, instead of scolding them and making them wary about handling money later.

Age-appropriate teaching

When children ask their parents 'Do we have a lot of money?' or 'Why can't we have xyz?', they're not always talking about money. The younger children are wondering why they can't have a toy or a vacation; the older children are wondering why their friend gets to do things they don't. Parents need to think about the question from the child's point of view, empathise and give an age-appropriate response.

Gender sensitivity

Children are also sensitive to gender biases. In many families, girls are taught about saving and budgeting, while boys are taught about investing and growing money. Most parents we interviewed stated that the husband makes the major financial decisions in the house. We often meet women whose husband, father or brother manages their investments. We can end this disparity by treating our children the same and ensuring that our daughter is as comfortable handling money and investments as her brother.

Now you're set. Good luck. Here's to raising financially independent children.

Parents' quiz

You and your partner should take this quiz separately and discuss your answers to develop a consistent approach to your child's financial education. The more aligned your values are, the more effective the message.

1. At what age should we start talking to our child about money?
    a. 6–10
    b. 10–12
    c. 13–16
    d. 16+
    e. When they become adults
    f. Talking to our child about money is not necessary, the child can learn on his/her own when he/she grows up.

2. What money-related mistakes did you make when you were younger that you do not want your child to repeat? (You can choose more than one answer.)
    a. Saving less
    b. Not investing
    c. Not paying my bills on time
    d. Taking on too much debt
    e. Spending more than my income
    f. Living too frugally
    g. Not giving back to the less privileged

    h. Other (specify)
    i. All of the above
    j. None of the above

3. What should we be teaching our child? (Select the ones you think are important.)
    a. How to shop for the best deal
    b. How to save regularly
    c. How to budget money
    d. How to protect personal financial information online
    e. How to pay bills
    f. How to check your bank statement/balance your chequebook
    g. How do credit cards work
    h. How taxes work
    i. How to invest and grow your money
    j. Giving to the less privileged
    k. All of the above
    l. None of the above, the child can learn on their own when they grow up

4. At what age should we share our income details with our child?
    a. < 10
    b. 10–18
    c. 18–25
    d. 25+
    e. Never

5. Should we involve our child in family budgeting/spending decisions? (Discuss specific examples, if that is helpful.)
   a. To a great extent, so that they can learn by doing
   b. Occasionally, when it makes sense
   c. It never occurred to me
   d. It is not appropriate

6. Should we give our child a monthly spending budget?
   a. Yes, that is how we plan our expenses and spend our money
   b. Yes, we don't have a household budget, but our child should learn
   c. No, our child can budget their expenses when they are older
   d. No, we should give our child everything we did not have when we were growing up

7. What should we do if our child asks for an expensive game that we know they will not use for long?
   a. Buy it. We should give our child everything we did not have when we were growing up
   b. Ask our child to justify the purchase and buy it if they have a good reason
   c. Don't buy it, but explain your decision to them
   d. Don't buy it and don't give an explanation

8. How should we deal with overindulgent grandparents who cannot say no to their grandchild?
    a. Do nothing. Grandparents should always be allowed to indulge their grandchild
    b. Talk to the grandparents and ask them not to overindulge their grandchild
    c. Talk to the grandparents and ask them to check with you before they buy anything expensive for their grandchild

9. At what age should we give our child a smartphone?
    a. 6–10
    b. 10–12
    c. 13–16
    d. 16+

Money Milestones

Use the chart below to keep track of your child's progress in their financial education journey.

Up to age 10
- Understands that money is a way to get things
- Understands where money comes from
- Knows how to pay for things and get change
- Understands value of some things
- Has the ability to wait for something she wants
- Understands the concept of borrowing and returning

Ages 10–15
- Understands that money is limited
- Understands the effort it takes to earn money
- Understands the difference between needs and wants
- Can track expenses
- Understands the downside of impulse buying
- Recognises the impact of peer pressure
- Understands the concept of investing
- Practises gratefulness and giving

Ages 15+
- Understands different careers in terms of earning potential
- Understands the process of comparison shopping
- Has the ability to plan for long-term goals
- Understands the importance of starting early when it comes to investing
- Understands the concept of credit cards and borrowing

2

Pocket Money or Not

'My budget is over. Can I get a new one?'
— Mira, age 9

Key Financial Habits

- Plan and stay within budget
- Practise self-control
- Track expenses
- Save regularly

You've already taken the first step towards your child's financial education. Here's to raising smart, caring and financially literate kids! Now take this short quiz to see where you are in this journey to help your kids develop good financial habits.

Your child's money journey: Are you on track?

1. How do your kids get spending money?
    a. Children don't need money. An adult is generally available to spend for them
    b. I give them money when they need it
    c. Allowance/Pocket money
2. How do you keep track of your children's spending?
    a. She can spend on whatever she wants. I give her total freedom
    b. I monitor her spending like a hawk
    c. She keeps track of her spending and I review it with her regularly

3. Where do your kids keep their money?
   a. With me
   b. A piggy bank, which they keep
   c. A bank account. I review the bank statement with them regularly

4. Do you talk to your kids about money?
   a. What's the rush? There is plenty of time to worry about money when they are adults
   b. Sometimes – I would like to, but I don't know what to say
   c. Regularly – children should learn about money

5. You decide to set up an investment account for your teenager. You:
   a. Pick the best companies to invest after careful research
   b. Let your child pick the companies and manage the investment account
   c. Do some research together and jointly decide what to buy

6. What mindset do you want your kids to have about money?
   a. Spend it while you have it
   b. Money can't buy happiness, but more money means more success
   c. Money is an important tool, so it should be managed carefully

Scoring

Give yourself 1 point for every A you have selected, 2 points for every B you have selected and 3 points for every C you have selected. Calculate the total points.

If your total points are:

15–18: Congratulations! You are an Involved Parent when it comes to teaching your kids about money. You are well on your way to helping your children develop good financial habits and building a good attitude towards money. You should use the tips and activities in the book to increase your kids' money management abilities and confidence.

10–14: Great! You are an Aware Parent when it comes to teaching your kids about money. You understand the importance of instilling good money habits in your children. You should use the techniques described in this book to talk to your kids about money and give them more tools to practise money management.

6–9: You are a Hands-off Parent when it comes to teaching your kids about money. As we have mentioned earlier in the book, research shows that money habits and attitudes develop at an early age.[1] You have taken the first steps to helping your children develop good money habits and attitudes by reading this book and taking this quiz. The next few chapters discuss activities to help you raise financially smart children.

Now that you know where you are in your child's financial education journey, let's start with the first tool to give your child hands-on experience: pocket money.

Why give your child pocket money

Can you really teach your child how to play football without a ball? Similarly, it's hard to teach a child about money and the value of money without giving them any money. Letting a child handle a small amount of money is a simple way to inculcate good money habits.

> **Research**
>
> Research shows that pocket money with parental control and explicit advice from parents increases the propensity to save by 16 per cent and the saving amount by 30 per cent.[2]

Pocket money helps kids learn and practise invaluable life lessons of saving, spending, budgeting and giving (donating). When kids start learning these lessons between the ages of 6 and 10, it has a threefold benefit:
1. Starting young helps drive the message and instil good financial habits.
2. Small mistakes will lead to big learnings.
3. Handling money will build confidence.

Pocket money, self-control and delayed gratification

A primary goal of giving kids pocket money is to teach them the balance between saving and spending. Saving is about discipline, delayed gratification and self-control. Does your child routinely ask for more chocolate or TV time? Believe it or not, your child's self-control may have something to do with their ability to save when they grow up.

Is self-control related to savings? Can self-control in the early years impact savings ability in the later years?

Researchers investigated the health and behaviour of 1,000 children, born in Dunedin, New Zealand, in 1972–73, over a 40-year period. The study found that the people who exhibited lower self-control as children were less likely to have saved money, owned their home and planned for retirement. Also, lower self-control during childhood had a strong correlation to lower credit scores (Dunedin study).[3]

When we compare our childhood to that of our kids, we are hard-pressed to find examples where kids have to really wait for something. We live in a world of instant gratification. As kids, if we wanted something, we would wait to go to a store, check if the item was in stock, and use physical cash to make the purchase. All of these things acted as small pauses between thought and action. Now, when we or the kids want something, we open a shopping app, find it online, click 'buy now', use digital money – in less than two minutes, the purchase is done. Almost magically, the item is at our doorstep the next day. With the advent of food apps and entertainment apps, our ability to delay gratification has become even worse. In these times, our self-control is the internal compass that puts a pause between thought and purchase.

So, can we help improve our child's self-control or is it purely genetic? Don't give up and throw in the towel just yet. The Dunedin study showed that self-control did improve for some of the participants as they became adults. Pocket money gives children an opportunity to exercise self-control from an early age as they make spending and saving decisions.

When to start giving pocket money

The short answer: Between ages 6 and 10.

The long answer: By age 6 or 7, kids can understand the concept of money. They understand that you need money to buy chocolate or cake or toys. Most kids will know when something costs a lot of money (a fancy toy, for example) versus when something costs less money (candy or lollipop). While they may still have abstract ideas about the value of money, they have a general sense of money. (*Soneera's note:* My child, age 7, asked me 'what is expensive?' a few days ago.)

If your child is older and you have not been giving pocket money, start now. Get your child into the habit of receiving some money every week, and being accountable for the money.

How much pocket money to give

This will vary based on where you live, what school your kids go to, and your income. But in general, for younger children, from age 6 onwards, we recommend giving between Rs 50 and Rs 100 per week. At this age they can track their pocket money as they have learnt basic addition and subtraction in school. Give them opportunities to spend the money, maybe at the school canteen or the stationery or grocery store. The kids will learn how much items cost and how to collect change correctly.

You can increase the amount as they grow older. If you aren't sure how much to give, you can include your kids in the decision-making process. If you know their friends' parents, you can decide the same amount for all the kids.

> **Research**
>
> Research shows 52 per cent of kids between 7 and 14 years get pocket money in metros. The average amount is Rs 555 per month.[4]

But what if their friends are getting a lot more money

Niru and Alok had this issue with their daughter, Anaya, when she was a teenager. She constantly asked for more spending money. Niru and Alok wanted Anaya to learn the value of money, so they refused to give in and give her more money.

This led to constant arguments, and eventually they had to see a counsellor. They recognized that the purpose of pocket money is to teach children financial responsibility and not to make them feel deprived. They spent some time with Anaya to understand her expenses, created a budget and increased her pocket money. They suggested cutting back on wasteful expenses, like eating out several times a week, but allowed other expenses. In fact, they gave her a little more so that she could save a small amount every month and build a saving habit. After the changes, Anaya felt empowered to make better spending and saving decisions. 'It was amazing to see her making financial choices and trade-offs that adults make every day, such as, "If I buy these shoes today, I can't go to the movies later with my friends",' reveals Niru.

But what if you do not have the ability to increase your child's pocket money? In that case, an honest talk explaining your financial situation would be a good way to handle the situation instead of just saying no. Psychologist Alaokika Motwane says 'explaining the cause and consequence to children is a good way to explain the situation'. You can explain that if you increase their pocket money (cause), you may not be able to spend as much on their postgraduate college education (consequence).

Keep in mind
- Deciding how much to give your child is a personal decision, based on your finances and your child's personality. Do not over-provide. Give enough that your child is comfortable. Giving too much means your child will never have to make tough decisions such as 'do I want this or that?'
- If you ask them to save from money they were spending anyway, they will resent you for making them save, and it will not be a 'fun' thing for them to do. So cover their expenses and give just a little extra to ensure that they get into the habit of saving.

How to give pocket money

Set an alarm on your phone, for every Sunday at 10 a.m., for example, or link the time of giving the pocket money to a weekly task that you do. Be consistent, be disciplined and make sure the money is dispensed weekly. If you do it monthly, it won't be a regular enough occurrence to drive the point home. Weekly allowance also helps kids track their spending, since they're only accountable for one week at a time, instead of trying to remember where they spent money 20 days ago.

Once you give the pocket money, help your child divide it into three jars or envelopes – Spend, Save and Give (Donate).

For example, if you have a child between the ages 6 and 8, and you've decided to give them Rs 100 a week, it would be divided as follows:

Spend   Rs 60
Save   Rs 20
Give   Rs 20

The most important point of this entire exercise is for your child to tangibly see cash accumulate in the jars/envelopes/piggy banks. As your children grow older (ideally around ages 10–12), open a bank account for them to start depositing their savings. The thrill of opening an account with money that they can call their own will be enough to get most children to start saving.

But my child doesn't spend any money!

We've heard this from many parents. If you truly feel this way, track your spending for a week – not just cash but even on commonly used e-commerce apps, or the time you took your child with you to the grocery store and they said: 'Can I please have a cupcake?' (*Soneera's note:* I used to feel the same way. My older child rarely asks for anything. But when I tracked my spending, I realised that I spent over Rs 1,000 on him on books every month. So now, I give him the same allowance that I would've spent on the books anyway and deduct the cost of the book from the jar when I make an

E-Reader purchase online. Similarly, a friend realised that she spent over Rs 5,000 a year at a well-known fashion store on 'extras' her daughter wanted, such as princess hair clips or sequinned socks.)

The point, we must stress, is not to make your child feel bad about their spending – it's just to make them realise that you are spending money. The next time you are at the mall, and your child asks for something small, like movie-themed hair clips or even a chocolate, pause and tell your child: 'Yes, sure, but this will come out of your spending jar.'

It is not that you can't buy the chocolate yourself or about affording it or making your child self-conscious about spending. The point is to instil a small sense of accountability and responsibility when it comes to spending money. So do go home and remove Rs 40 or how much you spent from the spending jar.

Yes, if your child has grandparents in the house, they may simply ask them for money to buy the chocolate or toy, but as long as parents are consistent in the way they give and regulate pocket money, your child will understand the bigger picture. (More on this in Chapter 4.)

Paying for household tasks

Many parents like to peg a child's pocket money to the work they do around the house or the marks they get in school. They believe that a child should 'earn' the money and not develop a sense of entitlement. We disagree.

We all do some work in the house, regardless of how privileged we are. You should not be paying your child for something they should be doing anyway, as a functioning member of the household. Your child should not clean up their room or get good grades because you're paying them to do it. They should do it without expecting compensation. Sure, if your child scores really well, you can reward the effort. But this should not be how your child 'earns' their pocket money.

Gift money

It's common practice in India for kids to receive 'covers' at birthdays and other family functions. Many parents take the money and deposit it in their child's bank account. But we recommend using these opportunities to teach your children valuable money lessons. Depending on the amount, you can guide them to save some of the money and spend the rest on something that they want. Let them spend it as they see fit. Yes, they will probably grow out of those expensive shoes or play with that game only a few times, but let your children make these choices and learn from them.

Monitoring pocket money

Once you start giving your children pocket money, will they automatically become financially responsible?

Honestly, no.

Giving them the money is not enough. Some level of parental supervision is important. In fact, research shows that pocket money with parental control and advice has a significant impact on the amount kids save when they become adults. However, giving pocket money without parental supervision does not have much impact on their saving behaviour when they become adults.[5]

The minute you give your child an allowance, you must give them a notebook (if they own a smartphone, you can download a budgeting app) so they can track their spending. (*Binal's note:* My child and I have formed a WhatsApp group called '*Hisaab*', where she accounts for her spending on a weekly basis. This helps her keep track of expenses and helps us keep an eye on our daughter's spending.) Don't be harsh on your child if they cannot account for all the money or if they make mistakes. We want our children to have a happy, healthy relationship with money. If children are terrified of making mistakes, they will not want to deal with money now or later.

Alternatives to pocket money

Many parents don't like giving pocket money for various reasons. Some believe that pocket money encourages entitlement and some believe that all money is common family money. Others believe that it will encourage kids to spend on unnecessary things and find it more convenient to give money on demand. This allows them to say 'no' to inappropriate expenses. In all these cases, the child is not getting an opportunity to handle money, make saving versus spending decisions, and build good financial habits.

Delnaaz and Zubin do not give their kids pocket money. They do not want the weekly hassle of giving and tracking pocket money. They want to know where the children are spending money and want the option to say 'no' if the kids want something unreasonable. But, they give their kids a spending budget when they travel. This provides their kids an opportunity to make spending choices within a limited budget. Their kids have to choose between the many souvenirs that are important at that moment, but forgotten the moment they return home. Of course their kids are not learning to save, but at least they are learning how to make spending choices. Similarly, you could give your kids a budget when you go on a shopping trip with them. It could be a trip to the stationery store or a more expensive trip to the mall. You could also give them a budget to buy a birthday gift for their friend. All these are opportunities to help them learn and make spending choices.

Pocket money gone digital

Many schools do not allow their kids to carry cash. Parents have to load money on an ID card and the kids can use this card for their canteen or stationery expences. (*Binal's note:* After my daughter's school made canteen/stationery

> **Research**
>
> Research shows we actually feel pain when we spend money. 'Tightwads' end up spending less than they want to because they feel intense pain while spending money. 'Spendthrifts' feel insufficient pain while spending, so they end up spending more than they would like to.[6]

payments digital, my daughter found it tougher to keep track of her spending and often spent more.)

Research shows that people tend to spend more on cards because they don't feel the pain of physically giving away cash.[7] Yes, people actually feel pain when they spend! It also takes the sting out of giving away crisp notes and the sight of an empty wallet. As your child grows older, give them pocket money (or some part of the money) in a mobile wallet or a prepaid card. This will help them get used to digital payments. The habit of tracking their money on paper (or digitally) will help them feel some of the pain of spending and keep them from overspending.

Pocket Money Road Map

- Start giving pocket money between the ages of 6 and 10 years.

- Start small (Rs 50–Rs 100 weekly) and increase it with their age. You can involve them in deciding how much they need.

- Divide the money into three jars/envelopes named Saving, Spending, Giving.

- Give them pocket money weekly and teach them how to track it (on paper or on the smartphone with an app).

- As they grow older, help them deposit their savings in their own bank account.

- Give them money on a prepaid card or a mobile wallet when they are older.

- Follow these same steps with gift money.

- If you choose not to give them pocket money, give them a spending budget on holidays and shopping trips.

Pocket Money or Not 35

Activities – With Younger Kids (ages 6–12)

Activity 1: Budgeting – Make spending choices to stay within budget

Arush is a 14-year-old boy and gets a monthly allowance of Rs 1,500 from his parents. His expenses are described below.

- Rickshaw to and from classes – Rs 600 (Rs 20 one way, for 15 classes. He can walk to the classes, but he is always late and has to take the rickshaw)
- Canteen expenses – Rs 300 (assuming every day it is Rs 15 daily for 20 days of school)
- Stationery items – Rs 100
- Mobile phone recharge – Rs 200
- Outings with friends – Rs 300 (three outings per month)

Arush's parents have asked him to save Rs 200 every month. How would he save this money?

(Note for parents: Use this exercise to help your child learn to prioritise expenses and make a budget.)

Activity 2: Prioritise expenses – Organise these expenses in order of your priority

- Food to sustain oneself – rice, roti, vegetables
- Food for fun – chocolate, sweets, ice cream
- House
- Vacation home
- Vacations

- Clothes/Shoes
- Party clothes/Shoes
- Toys/Games
- Phone
- iPad
- Laptop
- Internet

Money Tasks for Teenagers

Task 1: Planning a family vacation

Get them involved in planning the family vacation. Once you have decided the place together, let them help you with the research.

- Flight/Train options
- Accommodation options – 5-star, 4-star, 3-star and so on
- Activity options
- Restaurant options

Have them list out the expenses of the different options. Give them a reasonable budget. Let them choose the options based on the budget. Discuss the trade-offs that the family can make to stay within budget.

Task 2: Household budget

Share your monthly household budget with them. For example:
- Electricity (Rs 5,000)
- Staples such as rice, vegetables, milk (Rs 8,000)
- Internet (Rs 1,000)
- Eating out (Rs 5,000)
- Netflix/Other subscriptions (Rs 1,000)
- Movies and other entertainment (Rs 5,000)
- Salaries of household help (Rs 10,000)
- New toys/gadgets (Rs 5,000)

Total spend: Rs 40,000

1. Give them a budget of Rs 35,000 and ask them to list their priorities, on how they would balance needs and wants to stay within the budget.

2. Ask them to list some of the expenses missing from this budget such as school fees, insurance and annual subscriptions.

(Note for parents: Remember there are no right or wrong answers here. You can use these exercises to help your child learn to prioritise expenses.)

Money Talks – Curated Financial FAQs for money conversations with your children

Why can't we just go to the ATM when we want money?

The ATM is not our personal, unlimited money genie. The ATM allows us to access our deposits in the bank. If your bank balance is Rs 20,000 and you try to withdraw Rs 21,000, your transaction will be declined.

What is a budget?

A budget is a plan of how we will spend a fixed amount of money given to us over a fixed period of time. A vacation budget or a shopping budget, for example, caps the amount we can spend.

Why do I need a budget?

A budget helps us plan our expenses so that we can enjoy our present but also set aside some money for the future. Planning a budget and sticking to it will (ideally) prevent us from overspending.

Why can't I get the latest smartphone/ fancy game/ dinner at an expensive restaurant? or You have the latest smartphone/expensive bag. Why can't I have one too?

(*Note to parents:* There are different ways to address this.)

Why do you need it? Will the latest smartphone/bag make you happier? Do you want your worth or coolness or acceptance to be defined by a smartphone or bag?

OR

Every family has different values and priorities. Our family does not spend so much money on phones. We would rather pay more for books/experiences/family vacations. When you start earning you can decide what you'd like to spend on, but as a family, these are our priorities and our spending plan. (*Note to parents:* This may not work if your child sees you upgrading your phone every other year.)

OR

I bought this expensive bag after finishing my education and working very hard. This bag is not a necessity, but a hard-earned luxury that I've received at a much older age.

Why does dad give me money? Why not mom?

Every family is different. In some families, mom and dad work. In some families only one parent works. In our family, dad handles the money, so he gives you money.

Why do we need to save if we have enough money?

We may have enough to cover inflation but oftentimes we cannot estimate how much money we will need for sickness or medical emergencies. For example, no one could have predicted a complete loss of income due to the COVID-19 pandemic. We save because we cannot predict the future and we want to ensure that our lives and lifestyles are as safe and smooth as possible.

This pocket money is mine to spend. Why should I tell you where I spend it?

We give you pocket money to help you build good financial habits. Making good spending choices is one of these habits and we need to know where you spend to guide you better.

(*Note to parents:* Another philosophy is that children can spend where they want, and how they want, as long as they have tracked their expenses and can account for every rupee. Depending on your child's age and comfort handling money, you can decide which approach works for you.)

How much money do we have? How much do you earn?

(*Note to parents:* Once again, most children don't really want to know your net worth. They're asking you to find out something deeper – whether they're as rich as their friend, or whether they can aspire to have a certain lifestyle. Based on your child's age, ask them why they're asking this question and give an age-appropriate response.)

Let's not compare how much money we have to someone else. We have enough for our needs, and let us be thankful for what we have.

OR

When you are older and get a good understanding of money, I will share my income with you and also show you our savings/investments. For now, let's learn about money and show me that you can be responsible with money.

Expert Speak

How financial experts talk to their children about money

Anup Maheshwari, Joint CEO and Chief Investment Officer, IIFL Asset Management. He has two sons. One is studying Entrepreneurship at Babson and the other plans to pursue Veterinary Studies.

Bill Clinton's biography left a lasting impact on me. At the time my kids were too young, so I replicated it with my nieces. I gave them Rs 3,000 every month. I asked them to invest one third, spend one third and donate one third. They could spend their one third as they pleased, but they had to send me an email before the end of the month explaining which charity they donated their one third to and why, and which company they invested their one third share in and why. They had to research their chosen charity and investments. They didn't understand the significance of it at that age, but they learned the power of compounding pretty soon, and were amazed at how money grew. When my son went abroad to study, we gave him a fixed monthly budget, and he had to track his expenses.

Growing up, we talked a lot about business. How does a business make money? What is a balance sheet, profit and loss statement? And we always discussed real-life examples, like do you use Fevicol? Do you know which company makes Fevicol? Is it listed, what is the share price, how is it doing?

Investing in equity is the only way to compound capital and the beauty of investing is that your money works while you're sleeping. When it comes to kids, there is nothing like real experience; the more kids are involved in the investing process, the better they will learn. My son is 20 now and I always tell him to invest in what he knows. Long-term investing is key. Don't get distracted. Make mistakes but learn from them. Less activity, not more is the mantra of most successful investors.

Giving and investing are the two important lessons for our children. Sharing wealth gives a holistic approach to wealth creation and makes our children aware of their privilege.

3

Of Piggy and Other Banks

'Mom saves and I spend.'
– Tejal, age 13

Key Financial Habits

- Pay yourself first
- Save regularly
- Delay gratification
- Plan and set saving goals

In Chapter 2, we talked about pocket money and the importance of segregating that money into three sections – Save, Spend and Give. In this chapter, we talk about creative ways to inculcate the habit of saving.

Why teach our children to save

India has one of the highest savings rates in the world. Indians are savers. We saw our parents save and we save too. In fact, 72 per cent of the parents we surveyed say that they have taught their kids how to save money and 59 per cent of the kids save their money in a piggy

> **Survey**
>
> One in two parents wished that they had saved more when they were younger and they don't want their kids to repeat the same mistake

bank or a bank account. But are we doing enough to ingrain the saving habit in our children? With Indians spending more on everything, from buying more luxury goods to taking more vacations, our saving rate is falling. The Indian household saving rate has fallen from the 30s (per cent) to the 20s (per cent) over the last decade.[1]

As our kids grow up, saving will be a bigger challenge, with even more avenues to spend. Simply talking about saving will not yield results. We must give our children opportunities to save regularly. This will make them more likely to save when they start earning. Research shows that saving money in your adolescence will result in more saving as an adult.[2] It is all about developing a habit.

A child may ask you 'Why do I need to save at all?' or 'Why do I need to save now? I'll do it when I earn money', but explain to them that the goal is to help them develop a habit of saving and not contribute to the household savings.

So yes, you may be able to afford that giant toy at the toy store or the fancy new headphones, but having your child save and contribute towards them will help them learn important habits:

- Goal setting
- Delayed gratification
- Planning for the future
- Understanding the value of money

How to develop the saving habit

Pay yourself first

Most people think saving implies what is left over after spending their income. Even our kids save some of their gift money or pocket money after spending some of it. There is no plan and, therefore, saving becomes discretionary and inconsistent. The easiest and the best way to save is to do it first, instead of hoping there is money left over at the end of the month, i.e. 'pay yourself first'. So, if you give your kids pocket money, the 'saving' amount should be kept away as soon as they receive the pocket money. If your child receives gift money for birthdays and other festivals, together you can decide a saving amount to set aside before you take them to the mall to spend the rest of the money.

Have a plan

Planning is an important aspect of saving. Setting goals will motivate your kids to save and you can celebrate their success when the goal is achieved. As motivational speaker Brian Tracy says, 'Goals are the fuel in the furnace of achievement.'[3]

Here is what we suggest: Set up at least two saving goals every year for your children. These goals must be achievable in a fixed time frame. Goals can include anything they *really really* want, such as Lego, games to play on their gaming consoles, phone accessories, new shoes, or a watch. The kids don't need to fund the entire expense, you can make your child contribute Rs 2,000 towards a Rs 10,000 game, or Rs 500 towards a Rs 3,000 accessory.

Saving towards a goal helps children in multiple ways:
1. It will help them delay gratification. Instead of getting the game they want as soon as they ask for it, they will have to wait a few weeks/months before they get it.
2. Goal setting will motivate them to save and achieving their goals will motivate them to save more.
3. They will value the game more if they have helped pay for it.
4. They will learn the importance of planning for the future. For most kids/teenagers the future is 'Where will we eat tonight?' or 'When is our next trip to the movies?' Saving for the future is an abstract concept, but goal setting (and achieving) makes it real.

For older kids (above 10 years), discuss the concept of 'emergency fund' and its importance. The need for an emergency fund could not have been made clearer than during the COVID-19 pandemic and the ensuing lockdown in India. Many older kids understood the gravity of the situation and asked their parents about their family's finances – a topic that had rarely been discussed before. Shilpa, a mom we interviewed, revealed, 'About a month into our stay, my son Krishiv (17) came up to me and said,

"Mom, I know Dad's not working. All the factories are shut. How are we making money? Should we be worried?" It was good, because it gave us an opportunity to discuss our finances with him.'

How to encourage the saving habit

Saving should not feel like punishment – it should be something exciting that kids look forward to. Parents around the world have come up with very interesting ways to encourage their children to save. We've listed a few of these below.

Match their savings

This is optional, but when saving for a goal such as a new phone or an expensive toy, this one works really well. The next time your child asks you for something expensive, set a goal of 3–6 months, ask them to save and tell them you will match their savings. So, if something costs Rs 5,000, have them save Rs 500 over 5 months (Rs 2,500) and match that total. This will make the goal achievable. Achieving realistic targets helps increase your child's self-confidence, waiting for 3–6 months reinforces delayed gratification and that they've 'paid' for some part of it will make the purchase that much sweeter.

Pay interest on savings

This one is a little more complicated, but also a great way to introduce children to the concept of interest. (Keep it simple, don't compound just yet!) Paying interest on your child's savings adds value to their hard work and incentivises them to save more. As an added bonus, they will also learn maths concepts, such as calculating interest, very quickly. For example, if your child has saved Rs 100, consider giving them Rs 20 as interest or Rs 200 on the principal of Rs 1,000. Of course, 20 per cent interest rate is not realistic, but will get the point across.

Kevin O'Leary of Shark Tank used a transparent piggy bank for his children. Every night, when the kids were asleep he added money to the piggy bank as 'interest'. In the morning, the kids woke up and saw their money 'grow'.[4]

Start a competition

You can start a savings competition between your kids or with their cousins to encourage them to save. You can reward the child who saves the most or who can identify more ways to save money around the house. The idea is to learn through healthy competition.

A disclaimer though – you don't want to raise children obsessed with saving and reluctant to spend either. Talk to them about balancing their savings versus spending.

Where to keep their savings

For younger kids a piggy bank is good, so they can see their cash increasing. Buy an attractive piggy bank and place it where your child has easy access to it. For older kids (above 10 years), open a

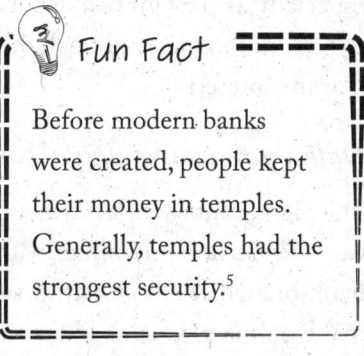

Fun Fact

Before modern banks were created, people kept their money in temples. Generally, temples had the strongest security.[5]

bank account. Let them fill in their own deposit slips and accompany you to deposit the money. Make a fixed deposit, even if it's for a small amount, so that children understand the concept of interest and passive income (more on this in Chapter 5). Talk to them about interest. Discuss the pros and cons of a piggy bank versus a bank account. Explain the cost and benefits of fixed deposits. (Don't worry, you don't have to research these financial products, we have listed simple points you can discuss with your children in the Money Talks section.)

With advances in technology, there are many other options to keep our savings.

Mobile wallets

Typically we use a mobile wallet account for spending, but it can also work as a safe and convenient way for your child to save and access their pocket money. You can get a mobile wallet account (like Paytm, Google Pay) for your child, especially as they grow older. Mobile wallets make it easier to give kids money and track their spending, but they do not pay any interest.

Online payments or digital bank account

The big advantage of a payments or digital bank is that you can open an account online, without making any trips to the bank branch. You can withdraw cash from the ATM and make online payments like a mobile wallet. The bank pays you interest but may cap the maximum balance.

Note: Both these methods require access to a smartphone, and not everyone accepts this form of payment.

Saving is not just about money

Saving doesn't have to be only in monetary terms. Unused resources are also savings. For example, have your child learn the benefits of saving electricity (going green), using less air conditioning or switching off lights when not in use and then track your electric bill over the next three months. They will notice a dip in the electricity bill and realise the importance of the saying – a rupee saved is a rupee earned. This exercise doesn't have to be restricted to electricity bills. There are many areas around the house where they can help you save, such as not wasting water, finishing food on their plate, or taking a doggy bag when there is leftover food in a restaurant.

The Piggy Bank Road Map

- Fix an amount to save from their pocket money and set it aside first, before spending.

- If you do not give them pocket money, decide how much to save from their gift money before they spend it.

- Set savings goals for contribution towards a big purchase.

- Get the younger kids a piggy bank to save their money and see it grow.

- Open a bank account for older kids (above 10 years of age).

- Review bank statements/passbooks with them to show them interest earned.

- Incentivise their savings habit by matching their savings, or paying them 'interest' on the money they save, or tapping their competitive spirit.

Activities – With Younger Kids (ages 6–12)

Activity 1: Discuss the following with your children

Why do adults choose a bank versus a piggy bank to keep their money?

_____
_____
_____
_____
_____

Why does a bank pay us interest?

_____
_____
_____
_____
_____

What are the costs and benefits of fixed deposits?

_____
_____
_____
_____
_____

Activity 2: Track savings – Create a passbook to keep track of your child's savings.

Piggy bank passbook

Date	Note	Deposit amount	Withdrawal amount	Balance

Money Tasks for Teenagers

Task 1: Open a bank account

Take your child to the bank to open a bank account. Here are some of the questions you should ask the banker:
1. How many types of savings accounts are there?
2. What is the interest rate on the savings account?
3. What are the minimum balance requirements for the account?
4. What are the fees charged?
5. Which account would you choose? Why?
6. What is a debit card?
7. How does a debit card work?
8. What are the fixed deposit rates?

Task 2: Make a deposit

Send your children to the bank to deposit their own savings. Let them fill the deposit slip and update their passbook. You can go with them the first few times, but then let them go regularly. As they visit the bank branch, they will learn more about different banking products.

Send them to deposit some cheques for you. Let them perform some of your banking errands. You may not want to share your bank balance with them, but you can certainly let them do simple tasks like depositing cheques.

Money Talks – Curated Financial FAQs for money conversations with your children

What are the pros and cons of a bank versus a piggy bank?

Banks keep our money secure. Imagine how much space and security we would need to keep all our money in cash at home or in piggy banks. Piggy bank money is available 24x7, but you have to go to the bank or an ATM to withdraw money. However, banks pay interest, so our money grows when we keep it in a bank. Piggy bank money does not grow.

What is interest?

Interest is what a bank pays us for our savings. For example, if the bank pays an interest of 5 per cent to open a savings account with them, we get Rs 5 every year for every Rs 100 we save and put in the bank. It's great! We don't have to do any work to earn this interest.

Why do banks pay us interest to keep our money safe? Shouldn't we be paying them? OR How do banks make money?

Banks make money from our deposits (we are the depositors). They loan the money we have kept in our account to a company or an individual (they are called borrowers). Banks lend the money to the borrowers at a higher interest rate compared to what they pay the depositors and keep the difference in the interest. For example,

Bank's income =
- Interest they charge the borrowers (8 per cent of Rs 10,000 lent to borrowers = Rs 800)
- − Interest they pay the depositors (6 per cent of Rs 10,000 of deposits = Rs 600)
- + Fees they charge both borrowers and depositors (Rs 200)
- − Costs (Rs 100)

Therefore, bank's income = Rs (800−600) + 200−100 = Rs 300

Is our money totally safe with banks?

No. If many of the bank's borrowers do not pay them back, then we can lose some of our deposits with the bank. But this happens very rarely because the government, with the help of the Reserve Bank of India (RBI), makes sure that banks keep enough money aside to pay back the depositors in case some borrowers don't pay them back.

What are fixed deposits? What are the costs and benefits of fixed deposits?

A savings bank account lets you deposit or withdraw money at any time. A fixed deposit locks in your deposit for a certain amount of time, for example, 30 days or 10 years. A fixed deposit generally pays a higher interest compared to a savings account, but you cannot use or withdraw that money until the lock-in period is over (unless you pay a penalty).

4

Shopping Trips and More!

'Mummy why don't you just print money and spend more?'
— Bhavesh, age 13

> **Key Financial Habits**
>
> - Differentiate between needs and wants
> - Control impulsive buying
> - Practise concious spending
> - Shop for value

Our children rarely see us save or invest, but they see us spend all the time – on groceries, school supplies, random online purchases. Our spending is very visible! Children learn by observing their parents, so conscious spending is the first step in encouraging healthy spending behaviour in our children.

Fun Fact

One-rupee or a higher denomination can be used to settle any given amount. However, a 50 paise coin cannot be used to pay any amount more than Rs 10.[1]

If we habitually buy expensive clothes or eat out, chances are, so will our child. 'You cannot walk into a store to buy rain shoes and come out with three sandals and then advise your child not to buy on impulse,' explains Desiré Dias, a

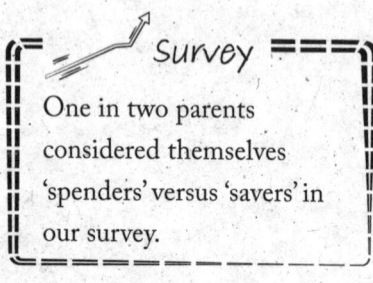

Survey

One in two parents considered themselves 'spenders' versus 'savers' in our survey.

child counsellor we interviewed. Whether expensive clothes and other luxury items fit into our shopping habits or not, here are the five spending values that we should discuss with our children:

1. Practise mindful spending
2. Do not spend to fit in with friends (peer pressure)
3. Spend within your means
4. Shop for value
5. Track your spending

How to help our kids develop these values

Shopping, both online and offline, is a great tool to help develop healthy spending behaviour in our children. We all remember our first lessons on money, when we went on shopping trips with our parents, to buy vegetables or clothes. When our children shop with us, and eventually alone, these are the questions they should learn to ask before making a purchase.

Do I need this or want this?

The first step is to teach children the difference between wants and needs. For example, children need food, shelter, clothing and education. Anything above these needs are wants. Explaining this difference to our children helps bring some perspective to their demands, and adds a pause between thought and purchase.

(Binal's note: At dinner one night, each of us listed the three things we'd want if we were stranded on an island. My husband and I thought of food, clothes and matches. My daughter said phone and the internet. She was okay living without food. We laughed, but I realised that wants and needs may be different across generations.) Being flexible while giving our children some perspective on wants versus needs is important. The next time your child absolutely 'needs' to spend money on something you don't understand (an expensive dinner or clothes) do not always say no. Give them some flexibility, or ask them to save more next time, or cut back on some other expense.

Do I have to have it now or can it wait? (or saying no to impulse shopping)

Our survey reveals that one in three parents gave money to their children almost every time they asked for it. Imagine getting something every time you asked – these are the stepping stones to entitlement. This may sound like common sense, but please say 'no' to your children. It's very important that kids hear 'no' occasionally, if not frequently. Even if you plan on getting something for them, practise saying 'not right now'. There are always occasions to look forward to – a birthday, a festival or an achievement. Delaying gratification is one of the most important factors for success in life. By constantly saying 'yes' to our children's every whim, we are again setting them up with unrealistic expectations, according to Georgia Manning, counsellor, psychotherapist and the director of Wellbeing For Kids.[2]

Delaying gratification helps instil discipline and patience; two key attributes that will help kids control impulse purchases as they grow older. 'Children need to have the experience of learning how to delay gratification and cope with the limits placed upon them. The resilience your children develop from such experiences lasts a lifetime, whereas the anger and upset they direct at you is only temporary,' writes Dan Mager in *Psychology Today*.[3]

Does this fit within my budget?

Give your children a budget for shopping. Help them evaluate the pros and cons of different items so that they don't always buy everything they like. (*Binal's note:* Our behaviour in the lockdown was a learning experience in budgeting. My daughter kept ordering things online every day, so I gave her a weekly shopping budget. Now it's no longer nail polish and toys, it's one or the other. She is questioning how much she will use something versus just buying it. She now looks at reviews, compares prices, and decides whether she needs it or not. I love spending time with her and helping her decide.)

Am I getting the best value possible for it?

Practising comparison shopping will help your children understand that shopping is not only about price, but also about value. Involve your child when you are making a big purchase, like a TV. Along with prices, discuss the pros and cons of features, brands and quality. It will help them realise the whys and hows of comparison shopping. Shopping for value forces us (once again) to add a pause between thought and purchase.

Conscious spending – Is my purchase environmentally friendly? Is it sourced at a fair price?

Spending is not just about us but also our environment and our planet. A bamboo toothbrush, for example, is 5x the cost of a plastic one, but a much better choice for the environment. In these cases, paying more may be justified. There are many other examples – organic clothing, purchases that directly benefit the farmer, greener appliances, electric cars and so on. Let children think about the consequences of their purchases and of fast fashion. (Is this something you will wear after this season? Will you want a new phone in 6 months when a new version releases?) Raising conscious children is the need of the hour.

How to help our children deal with peer pressure – online and offline

(Soneera's note: I remember when I was in Class 3, more than half my class had the Cello Squeezie water bottle and I wanted it too. Peer pressure starts from a very young age and is not always about the big things. Technology and

social media make it more pervasive than it was for our generation.)

Talking to children from a young age helps them deal with peer pressure. Help them understand that free social media apps make us the product, and marketers will try and sell all kinds of things to us. 'I always tell my children and my clients that what you see about a person (a friend or an influencer) on social media is (a) a very small fragment of their life, (b) that may or may not be true, and (c) it's what they want you to believe. And when children really absorb the meaning of all three parts of that sentence, it really gives them a healthy perspective on what they consume on social media. Be a conscious consumer of the internet,' explains life coach, Dr Shweta Aversekar. These conversations will help children view what they see on social media with healthy scepticism. Characters and situations on television shows and movies are also a great way to explain some of these ideas to your children and discuss topics like peer pressure, relationships, and positive self-image.

When your child wants something 'because their friends have it', do not dismiss them. Alaokika Motwane, a psychotherapist, says: 'Have an open discussion and ask them to justify their reasons. Help them understand the true reasons for why they want to purchase the item – is it genuine want versus peer pressure–influenced want? If you don't agree with their request, explain why. Tell them that things don't define them and won't make them 'cool'. If you can't afford the item, tell them you are saving money for their education or a family vacation. If you don't think the item is value for money, tell them just that. They may throw a tantrum and say 'I hate you', but they are only testing your limits. Be gentle and hold firm. After a few battles they will come around.' Depending on what they want, you may want to compromise. Let them achieve something like do well in school to 'earn' the item.

Do you recognise financial peer pressure?

Take this quiz to find out if your child is susceptible to peer pressure.

1. Does your child bring up what their friends are doing (going to so and so restaurant or to so and so place) in conversation?
    a. Frequently
    b. Sometimes
    c. Rarely
    d. Never

2. Does your child ask you questions such as 'Why can't we have a fancier car or bigger house?'
    a. Frequently
    b. Sometimes
    c. Rarely
    d. Never

3. Does your child ask you for more money because all their friends are headed some place expensive?
   a. Frequently
   b. Sometimes
   c. Rarely
   d. Never

4. Does your child spend money on 'treating' their friends or paying for them?
   a. Frequently
   b. Sometimes
   c. Rarely
   d. Never

5. Does your child spend money on friends with the expectation that they will not repay it?
   a. Frequently
   b. Sometimes
   c. Rarely
   d. Never

6. Does your child ask for the latest gadget or toy/game or accessory?
   a. Frequently
   b. Sometimes
   c. Rarely
   d. Never

Scoring:
Frequently = 4 points, Sometimes = 3 points, Rarely = 2 points, Never = 1 point
20–24: Your child is likely susceptible to peer pressure
13–19: Your child may be susceptible to peer pressure
<13: Your child may not be very susceptible to peer pressure

A note on smartphones

What is the right age to give your child a cell phone? Bill Gates did not give his kids a smartphone till they were 14.[4] Most of the parents we surveyed gave their kids a smartphone between the ages of 8 and 15. On average, kids received a smartphone when they were around 13 years old. Even if you give your child a smartphone, you can use apps like Google Family Link to monitor and limit your child's screen time and track app usage. Some parents prefer to monitor their child's screen time physically, some prefer that kids start self-monitoring, especially as they grow older. There are no right or wrong answers but limiting screen time will automatically limit outside influences.

As your children spend more time online, safety becomes an important issue. Use this chart to teach them about online safety.

Online safety – Keeping your money safe

B
Beware
of the unknown. Don't open emails, files and pictures from unknown sources.

E
Examine
links. Don't assume links from emails, messages or ads are genuine.

S
Share
with care. Don't give passwords, PIN numbers, identity documents to anyone.

A
Access
securely. Do not use a public computer or connection to access financial websites.

F
Filter
fake communication. Check for suspicious emails and websites asking for personal data.

E
Evaluate
your sources. Check information before you believe it. Is the person or website accurate?

What if my child really, really wants _____?

We've all had a child who saw a friend's toy or sneakers or some indulgence and came home and asked us, pleaded with us, begged us, tormented us for something really ridiculous, like Rs 10,000 sneakers or a rainbow-coloured glitter bag.

What we recommend is to set a middle ground or a benchmark. Choose a store you frequent, or the brand you buy most on an e-commerce site. Then check the price for a similar item in that store. So, if a T-shirt at your go-to clothing store is Rs 399, and the T-shirt your child wants is Rs 999, then tell them that you're willing to give them Rs 399 towards the T-shirt, and they can save the remaining Rs 600 from their pocket money. Alternatively, you could pay for half and ask your child to save for the rest from their pocket money.

Another option of dealing with your child's extravagant request is to ask them to justify the purchase, so there's an extra layer of thought instead of pure acquisitiveness. Ask them to make a pros and cons list for the item, listing all the reasons you should get it for them. Ask them to think about how much use they will get out of the item (will they grow out of it by next year, for example?). The point isn't to make kids grovel for their purchases, but to raise mindful spenders.

Mindful spending isn't just about money. For example, Rajiv and Shreya were happy to get a dog for their daughter Kareena but they wanted her to really grasp the responsibilities of owning a dog. They had her make a PowerPoint presentation on why they should buy her a dog, what would be the repercussions and responsibilities involved. 'I think it's very easy for kids to talk in abstracts, like, oh Papa, I'll walk the dog every day. Putting it down in a PowerPoint presentation helped Kareena understand what a big commitment it was and how much we would all have to do,' says Rajiv.

The lost water bottle problem

Your child has come from school or tennis or the park and there is no water bottle in sight. For the third time. In two months. It's not about the cost of a water bottle. It's the sense of responsibility – which is another reason the spend jar comes in useful, even if your child spends little or no money. The next time your child loses a bottle or snack box, deduct some money from their spend jar. Even a child as young as six doesn't like the thought of having to shell out money towards a replacement bottle.

Why we should ask our kids to track their spending

Expense tracking is the first step to raising awareness on where you spend your money. A parent we interviewed wished they'd discussed tracking spending and budgeting before their daughter went abroad for college. 'Aditi was always running out of money. We asked her to do some cost cutting, but she had no idea how to do it. When we finally listed her expenses, she realised that she'd go to the mall to hang with friends and shop impulsively – a purse here, a belt there. She started carrying less cash and automatically reduced her spending,' shares Tejal, Aditi's mother. Knowing where you spend is the first step in creating a reasonable spending budget and setting realistic savings goals.

Discussing budget cuts with your child

Parents we interviewed often expressed concern about discussing sensitive topics with children, such as job loss or budget cuts. Each situation is unique, depending on the gravity of the cut and amount of savings. But first, the partners should reach a consensus on how much they want to disclose. Second, be upfront with children. Don't let children pick up snippets of conversations (or worse, fights) around the house. 'When my father quit his job and took some time to figure out what he wanted to do next, my mother sat us down. I was in Class 8, my brother was in Class 10. My father was very patriarchal and didn't want us to be involved in money things, but mom disagreed. She said we are okay, we have savings, but please think twice before you ask for things until papa gets a new job. And we will make a few cuts to our lifestyle, such as fewer dinners or movies out,' reveals a parent from our survey. 'It's been 20 years but even today, I appreciate her honesty and strength.'

It is difficult to control my child's spending because the grandparents say yes to everything

Richa doted on her kids but she was a strict parent. Every time Richa said no, she'd find them eating chocolate or watching TV anyway and they'd say, but dada–dadi said yes. 'How can I teach my kids the value of money when the grandparents are doling out gifts and chocolate on demand?' she asked.

Grandparents love indulging their grandchildren. It brings them joy, it brings our children joy and the only villain in this process is the parent! But it doesn't have to be that way. 'I always tell my clients to see things from the grandparents' point of view. Their intention is not to ruin your parenting model. They are just trying to enjoy and love your child,' explains Dr Aversekar.

Psychotherapist Motwane concurs: 'If your grandparents meet your child once a week or once a month and spoil them on that day, and you are consistent for the remaining 26 or 29 days of the month, your child will not be affected by these indulgences. Consistency from the parents is key.'

If you have grandparent indulgence issues on a daily basis, then explain to them that you are trying hard to inculcate discipline and the value of money in your children and giving children gifts or spending money or sweets every day is not helpful. However, let them know that you see their point of view, and know that they love your child, and ask them to consider a compromise on the topic.

- One idea is to provide the grandparents with alternatives. Shweta, a mother we interviewed, reached a compromise with her in-laws when she substituted chocolate every day for organic lollipops twice a week. You can do something similar. Tell your parents or in-laws that instead of giving the child a toy, they may give gifts such as books, puzzles, and educational toys. Minal, another mother we spoke to, talked about how she convinced her mother-in-law with a green thumb to buy a new plant for her son every week – watering and taking care of it became an activity for both of them.

- Ask the grandparents to place a budget on how much they will spend on the child. This will not ruin their joy of giving something to their grandkids, but it will help you feel more in control of what and how often your child receives a gift. If they want to give an expensive gift, ask them to wait for a special occasion or event, so children learn delayed gratification.
- Ask them to spend time hanging out with children, instead of shopping. Ask them to share their stories of hardship and how they managed things in their days, or even stories from the classics. Alternatively, ask them to play simple games like Uno or carrom. 'My father was so excited to teach my daughter chess. It's been the best bonding experience, and watching them has been so joyous for me,' shares Mehul, a father we spoke to.

Note: For every parent that complained about a grandparent who was overindulgent or too judgemental, we also spoke to parents who were thankful for the role their parents played in raising their children.

Spending Road Map

- Use shopping experiences, both online and offline to teach your kids how to
  - Differentiate between needs and wants
  - Control gratification, avoid impulse shopping
  - Spend within budget
  - Shop for value
  - Align spending with values
- Have conversations about social media influencers and marketers.
- Use characters and situations in TV shows and movies to give examples of peer pressure.
- Make them justify larger purchases, listing the pros and cons.
- Limit screen time when they are younger, help them self-regulate when they are older.
- Make them track their expenses.
- Be upfront about money-related issues like job losses or salary cuts.

Activities – With Younger Kids (ages 6–12)

Activity 1: Smart or not smart

Life is all about choices we make. Discuss these choices with your child and decide whether these choices are smart or not smart.

1. Buying a vada pav from canteen every day.
2. Saving money from pocket money to buy a birthday gift for a friend.
3. Getting up late in the morning and missing the school bus and going by autorickshaw.
4. Buying cheap shoes online for a school trek instead of quality sportswear.
5. Carpooling with friends for music class.
6. Buying branded art marker pens for one time use instead of regular art marker pens.
7. Borrowing books from the library instead of buying new ones.
8. Waiting for an end-of-season sale to buy your clothes.
9. Saving some amount of pocket money for emergencies.
10. Buying regular stationary items from a store which gives you a discount versus a store that is closer to home.

Activity 2: Track your expenses

Track your expenses journal

Date	Description	Need/Want	Amount	Balance

Activity 3: Which smartwatch would you buy?

An exercise in comparison shopping. Don't forget to discuss value for money.

	Smartwatch 1	Smartwatch 2	Smartwatch 3	Choose
Cost	Rs 15,000	Rs 10,000	Rs 5,000	Need/Want
Features				
Waterproof	Yes	Yes	Yes	
GPS	Yes	No	No	
Heart rate monitor	Yes	No	No	
Call/Text	Yes	Yes	No	
Plays music	Yes	Yes	No	
Games	Yes	Yes	No	
Timer	Yes	Yes	Yes	
Fitness tracker	Yes	No	No	
Social media	Yes	No	No	
Long-lasting battery (24+ hours)	Yes	No	Yes	

Money Tasks for Teenagers

Task 1: Trips to restaurants/Ordering in

Let your teenager order. Let him/her check the bill and pay for the delivery. Similarly, before you pay the bill at a restaurant, let them check it.

Task 2: Household bills

Let your teenager write the cheques to pay your household bills. Let them learn how much you pay for electricity, water, groceries, and maintenance every month.

Task 3: Comparison shopping

Involve your teenager when you shop for a new appliance, TV, or computer for your new house. Let them do all the research and create a table like the one shown in Activity 3. Discuss the costs and benefits of all the options with them.

Money Talks – Curated Financial FAQs for money conversations with your children

Why can't we print more money and spend that?

History has shown us that just printing more money generally leads to inflation, which means prices will rise and the value of money goes down. In other words, if the government prints more money, we may earn more, but we will have to spend more to maintain the same lifestyle (because everything will cost more).

Why can't we spend all our money, why do we have to save? **OR** *What's the point of saving now and spending in my 40s or 50s? Now is more fun.*

Spending is for our pleasure and comfort now. Saving is for pleasure and comfort later. If we cannot earn in the future due to job loss, disability, or economic downturn then our savings will help us maintain our future lifestyle.

Life is a balancing act between spending and saving, fun and boring, healthy and junk and so on. Spend now, enjoy your 20s and 30s (they don't come back), but spend wisely and save for your future too.

What is expensive?

When a certain item costs more than what we usually spend on it, we may consider it to be expensive. For example, we typically spend Rs 500 per person at a restaurant. But if we go to a restaurant that charges Rs 1,000 per person, we may consider it to be expensive.

Expensive is a relative term. It depends on your lifestyle. For some people designer clothes are part of their daily lifestyle, but for others they may be expensive. It also depends on what a person values. For example, someone training for a marathon may be willing to pay more for a pair of running shoes, but someone else may find the shoes expensive.

Why do some things cost more and some things cost less? Why can't everything cost Re 1?

Some things cost a lot more to make. For example, a phone costs more than a book because the electronics in a phone cost more than it does to print a book. Sometimes certain brands demand a premium price. This could be because the brand looks better or is of better quality or will last longer or has more features. For example, a pen may cost more because it is better quality or lasts longer.

Expert Speak

How financial experts talk to their children about money

Zarin Daruwala, CEO, Standard Chartered Bank, India. She has a son and a daughter, both in their 20s. One is a lawyer and the other an engineer.

When the kids were in school, I gave them a small amount of pocket money, which they mostly spent on food. I did not have to worry about peer pressure or extravagant spending habits since their school, Bombay Scottish, encouraged a good value system. Children were not allowed to bring too much money to school and birthday parties and other events were not extravagant.

Even though both my children were raised with the same values, their attitude towards money is very different. My daughter likes to spend more than my son, who is conscious about saving. When my son was young, he would ask us to save his gift money in a bank account, but my daughter was not always inclined to do so.

After our son started earning, we connected him with an investment adviser. We ensure that he attends regular meetings with the adviser and learns to invest. After a bit of encouragement, our daughter has started investing in bank FDs and mutual funds. I feel that I should have encouraged my children to learn more about investing when they were younger, through courses on different types of investment products like stocks and mutual funds.

As soon as our children were old enough, we have been transparent with them about the details of our finances. I have observed that when you start involving your children in your finances, they automatically start taking interest. My husband and I prepared a will in our 30s, which we updated later. It is essential to keep in a secure place the details of one's assets and the various passwords and make them accessible to your children so that in an unfortunate event, the children are aware of what are the assets and what is the way forward.

Very often due to lack of will or non-transparency with the children, the money lying in the bank account lies unclaimed. It is our duty, as parents, to explain the details of our assets to our children and how they can gain access to these assets when we are gone. Many families have learnt this the hard way during the pandemic.

5

Grow Your Own Money Tree!

'My parents are discussing shares but I don't like sharing.'
— Jiaan, age 6

> **Key Financial Habits**
> - Understand investment basics
> - Invest and review regularly
> - Increase investing knowledge

What is the most important thing when it comes to growing your money? Knowledge of the stock market? No. Financial background? No. In-depth understanding of investment categories? No. The answer is TIME! Time is the most important factor when it comes to growing your money (more on this later). We may not have investment expertise, but the one thing we all have is time. Especially our children! Investing at an early age will help our children use the gift of time to reap greater rewards later in life. In fact, investing was the top concern among the 500-plus parents we surveyed.

Some of the parents we interviewed were savvy investors, but didn't know how to introduce their children to investing. Some didn't invest themselves, and hence

> **Survey**
>
> Fifty-eight per cent of the parents wished they had invested earlier and did not want their kids to repeat the same mistake. Seventy-seven per cent wished they had learned more about investing as teenagers.

didn't feel comfortable teaching investing to their children. In this chapter, we share simple ways to introduce children to investing. Any parent, with any level of investing knowledge, can use these games, activities and conversations to teach their kids about investing.

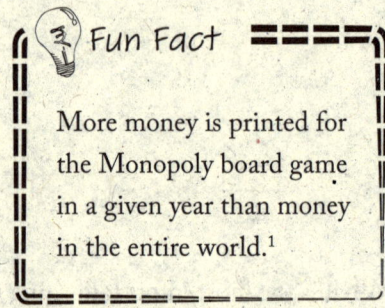

> **Fun Fact**
>
> More money is printed for the Monopoly board game in a given year than money in the entire world.[1]

What are the fundamentals of investing that our children must learn

As parents our role is to stress the importance of investing and give our kids hands-on experience, so they can absorb and appreciate the following fundamentals.

Saving money for the future is not enough!

Most of us teach our kids the importance of saving. But saving alone is not enough because inflation decreases the value of our savings. (*Binal's note:* 'My parents paid Rs 40,000 for 4 years for my engineering college fees in 1992. The same college now costs Rs 4.5 lakh for 4 years. This is a 9 per cent annual increase in fees.

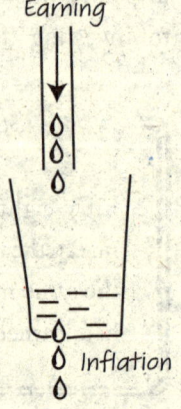

Inflation is a savings-eating monster!). If your savings don't grow faster than inflation, your spending will have to decrease (and honestly, when does that ever happen?). You can use a bucket analogy to explain this concept to your children. Imagine your savings as a full bucket of water, and then imagine inflation as a small hole in the bottom of that bucket. You can keep saving by adding more water, but some of those savings will leak away because of the 'inflation' hole. To maintain the full bucket, you have to fill it faster than the leak. Which brings us to the next principle – money makes money.

Money makes money

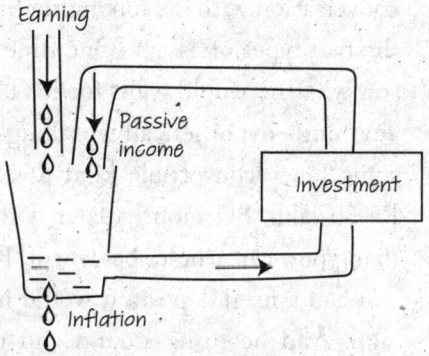

Most of us have two types of incomes – active income and passive income. Active income is income you have to work for (from job, salary, or business) while passive income is the income that you make from your investments (interest, dividend and rent). It's the money that your money makes! Passive income is the key to growing your money. 'If you don't find a way to make money while you sleep, you will work until you die,' explains the respected investor Warren Buffett.[2] Using the bucket analogy again, passive income lets us multiply and grow some of our savings to fill the bucket faster than the inflation leak. Passive income is what will keep you ahead of inflation. It is the money tree that will keep giving!

Choose your assets wisely!

To create passive income, you must own assets that increase in value faster than inflation. In a workshop we did for 15–16-year-olds at an elite Mumbai school, we asked kids to list their most important assets. Most chose phone or laptop. Yes, these are assets, but their value 'depreciates' over time and they do not generate passive income. However, 'appreciating' assets like land, equity/stocks and gold increase in value over time and generate passive income. Apurva's conversation with his son highlights the difference between the two types of assets. 'One time I asked my 16-year-old son what he would want for his birthday if he could have anything – hypothetically speaking of course. And he wanted some fancy convertible kind of car that costs more than Rs 50 lakh. Six months later, I told him in conversation that your car would be worth Rs 40 lakh now, but if you had a fixed deposit, it would have been worth Rs 51.5 lakh. And he turns around and tells me, "Yeah but you can't put a price on the fun I would've had. YOLO, Dad, YOLO." I had to look up YOLO. You Only Live Once. I'm still at a loss for words.' Depreciating assets give us pleasure and utility for now, but appreciating assets help us enjoy our future. This doesn't mean that we should never aspire to buy an expensive bag or an exotic vacation. The idea is to balance owning assets for consumption and pleasure now versus 'boring' assets that will enable us to enjoy our future.

Time is money, literally

If you were given two choices – taking Rs 1 lakh today or taking Re 1 that doubled every day over the next 30 days, which one would you pick? Most people would choose Rs 1 lakh today, but if you picked Re 1 doubling every day over 30 days, you would have been a crorepati, worth Rs 107 crore. At the beginning of the chapter, we had said that time is the most important factor that can help you grow your wealth. Time compounds wealth. And more time can compound your wealth dramatically.

Albert Einstein reportedly said that 'compounding is the most powerful force in the universe'. Our children learn to calculate compound interest in school, but can they appreciate how powerful the force of compounding is?

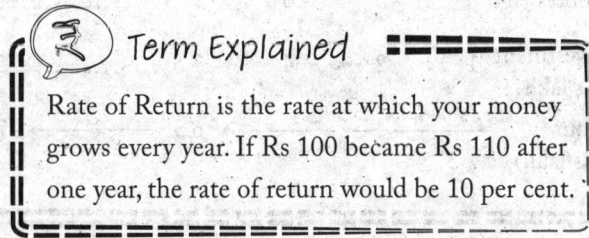

> **Term Explained**
>
> Rate of Return is the rate at which your money grows every year. If Rs 100 became Rs 110 after one year, the rate of return would be 10 per cent.

A simple way to help your children appreciate the power of compounding is the Rule of 72. This rule helps you calculate the approximate number of years it would take to double your money, given a rate of return. The approximate number of years to double is 72 divided by the rate of return. For example, at a rate of 25 per cent, you can double your money in approximately 3 years (72 divided by 25). In another 3 years, you would have doubled it again and made about 4 times your money, and in another 3 years you have doubled that and made approximately 8 times. (The actual number is closer to 7.5 times). If you invested Rs 1 lakh when your child was born, at a 25 per cent rate of return, you would have about Rs 7.5 lakh (a gain of about Rs 6.5 lakh) when they turned turned 9. In another 9 years when your child turned 18, your investment would have multiplied another 7.5 times and you would have Rs 55 lakh (a gain of about Rs 47.5 lakh). The illustration below shows how the gain increases dramatically from the first 9 years to the next 9 years of your child's life. That is the magic of compounding.

Child's Age	0	3	6	9	....	18
Investment (Rs lakh)	1	2	4	7.5	....	55
Gain (Rs lakh)			→	6.5	→	47.5

Research has shown that households that underestimate the power of compounding tend to save and invest less and borrow more.[3] The earlier our children start appreciating the power of compounding, the earlier they will start investing and use time to compound their wealth. Here is another story that you can discuss with your children.

The Story of Sara and Shanaya

Sara and Shanaya started working when they were 23. Both had similar jobs and made the same amount of money. Sara's parents had stressed the importance of investing from an early age and so Sara started investing as soon as she started earning, at age 23. On the other hand, Shanaya's parents had not taught her about investing and so she had to learn on her own and started investing a little later, at age 26. They both invested Rs 2,000 every month. The graphic on p. 96 illustrates their investment journey.

By starting only 3 years earlier than Shanaya and investing Rs 72,000 more, Sara's investment is worth almost Rs 14 lakh more at age 40. If they continue investing the same Rs 2,000 every month till age 60, Sara's investment would be worth almost Rs 5 crore more, only because she started investing 3 years before Shanaya. That is the power of compounding! *(The example assumes 18 per cent rate of return on investment.)*

Of all the money habits we hope to inculcate in our children, this is probably the most crucial when it comes to growing their wealth. We cannot stress the importance of starting early. Investing is about holding good assets and letting time work its magic!

Story of Shanaya and Sara

Shanaya	Sara
Started at age 26	Started at age 23
Invested Rs 2,000/month	Invested Rs 2,000/month

At age 40

Shanaya	Sara
Total invested = Rs 3.6 lakh	Total invested = Rs 4.3 lakh
Value of investment = Rs 18.1 lakh	Value of investment = Rs 31.9 lakh

At age 60

Shanaya	Sara
Total invested = Rs 8.4 lakh	Total invested = Rs 9.1 lakh
Value of investment = Rs 6.9 crore	Value of investment = Rs 11.8 crore

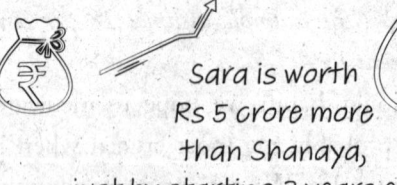

Sara is worth Rs 5 crore more than Shanaya, just by starting 3 years earlier!

Assumes 18 per cent annual return on investment

There's no such thing as a free lunch

One of the most common questions that college students ask us when we talk to them about money is: 'Ma'am, what should I invest in so that I can double my money quickly.'

All assets are not created equally. Some give a higher return, and the promise of making money quickly. But these assets are riskier and can lose money even quicker. For example, the meteoric rise of Bitcoin has attracted many young investors. Bitcoin rose from $35,000 in January 2021 to $60,000 in April 2021, but dropped down to $35,000 by May 2021. So you could have made or lost a lot of money depending on when you bought and when you sold. With all the ups and downs in its price, this digital currency is a risky asset. Many young investors are lured by the dream of fast money and unbelievable payouts with risky assets, only

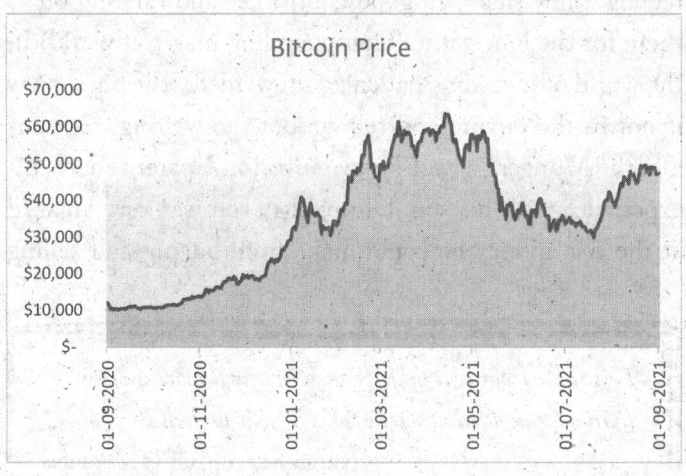

Source: https://finance.yahoo.com/[4]

to lose all or part of their investment. An important lesson is that risk and return go hand in hand – any asset that promises a high return will have high risk.

Patience pays!

Many families do not invest in the stock market because they believe that trading in shares is like gambling. 'My father thought the stock market was like gambling. I had to wait till I was 50 to start investing!' explains Bhavin, a father we interviewed. In a way, Bhavin's father is right. History shows that most people lose money in the long term by continuously buying and selling shares (short-term trading) because even the smartest investor cannot always 'time' the market and guess whether the share value will rise or fall in the short term. Most successful investors make money by buying a few shares in good companies and holding on to them for the long term. (Compounding magic at work!) In the world of investing, patience is rewarded. 'The big money is not in the buying and selling, but the waiting,' explains Charlie Munger[6], a well-known investor. A parent shares his experience with his son, Dhruv: 'My son was very amazed at the free money he could make from buying and selling

---

Less than 1 per cent of active traders earn more money than a bank fixed deposit over a 3-year period.

– Nithin Kamath, CEO, Zerodha[5]

stocks, when he discovered the stock market. Initially he made Rs 20,000 here, Rs 25,000 there. Then once or twice some big bets went wrong and all his profits were wiped out. He needed to learn that lesson for himself – I told him that investing wisely was about holding on to good, solid stocks of strong companies for a long period. He couldn't focus solely on buying and selling on a weekly basis.'

Now that we've covered the fundamentals of investing – it brings us to our next question.

How to help our children understand these fundamentals

Talking to them is one way. But showing them is even better.

Play games

When they are young (ages 8–14), games are a good way to teach them some of these fundamentals. For example, the Monopoly board game teaches many lessons in investing. See figure on p. 100.

In the Game of Life board game you make career and investment choices that can determine the outcome of the game. The game teaches you that making good financial choices and investing early in life can help build a strong future.

While playing these or other games with your kids, discuss the lessons learned. Help them understand the consequences of their decisions and how they impacted the outcome. Discuss how similar decisions are made in real life.

> ## Lessons from Monopoly
>
> - Saving is not enough. If you 'invest' in assets like property versus 'save' money in cash, you may be worth less initially, but will eventually end up richer.
>
> - Planning for emergencies. Hold some 'emergency' cash to pay your dues, like rent or taxes. Without this contingency money, you may end up mortgaging properties to borrow money.
>
> - Risk and return go hand in hand. The more expensive properties give you a higher return. But the higher investment in these properties also decreases your cash in hand, which may be needed to pay your dues (higher risk).
>
> - Patience pays. You cannot win right away; you have to own properties, build the hotels and wait for people to come to your properties for you to grow your wealth and win the game.

Show them

When kids learn how to calculate compound interest in school, you can give them examples like the ones we have shared to explain the power of compounding. But a better way would be to show them the power of compounding at work. Open an investment account for your child when they are born (or now, better late than never). Invest in mutual funds or shares, whatever you are comfortable with. After age 12, review these investments every 3–6 months. Seeing their money grow will help them understand the power of compounding. (*Binal's note:* I invested Rs 10,000 in a mutual fund in my daughter's name when she was 2 years old. Now she is 13 and the investment is worth Rs 50,000 – a return of over 15 per cent per year! I shared the statement with her when she turned 13. The 5x increase in her investment left a very strong impression on her. I will continue sharing the progress of her portfolio with her so that she understands the power of compounding.)

Give them hands-on experience

When kids are between 12 and 16 years old, introduce them to the stock market. Explain how owning a share makes you part owner of the company. They may be too young to understand valuation and financial statements, but you can use the legendary investor Peter Lynch's principle of 'invest in what you know'.[7] For example, all children like to eat at Domino's or Burger King or McDonald's. Ask them which of these three stocks they would like to invest in. They can do their own research. Which is more popular with their friends? Which one uses incentives or good marketing messages to attract customers? Which one offers better value for money? Invest in the company they choose and review the value of your investment regularly. If your child likes cars, you could ask them if they would like to invest in shares of Maruti Suzuki. Let them buy stocks based on products they use every day and build their own portfolio. This engagement will encourage them to proactively learn more about these companies.

They can create a portfolio with real or virtual money. If you plan to create one with real money, you can open a separate trading account in their name, with you as the guardian. If you are uncomfortable with teens creating a portfolio with real money, you can also create one with virtual money on some websites. Real money will get them more engaged, but virtual money will also help them experience the process of investing. Do a weekly or monthly review of their portfolio, depending on the time you have, to show them how markets move up and down in the short term.

Let them invest a small amount

When they get older, 18–19 years, open an account for them and give them some real money to invest and even make mistakes. Small mistakes will not cost much but lead to big learnings. Review their portfolio with them regularly.

I taught them the fundamentals of investing. Now what?

Investing is about continuous learning. Once your kids understand and appreciate the fundamentals of investing, don't stop! Continue their investing journey, via online and offline resources and courses that will help them increase their knowledge and experience. They can explore other avenues of investing, such as cryptocurrency, real estate, futures and gold.

I don't know anything about the stock market. How can I review their investments?

If you are uncomfortable reviewing their portfolio with them, have them review it with someone in your family or circle of friends who has more knowledge and experience. Your role can be just to encourage your children to invest and maybe even learn with them.

My child is happy eating burgers from Burger King, but couldn't care less how the company makes money.

That is okay. Investing in the stock market does not interest everyone. In fact, you will have many friends and family members who give their money to someone else to manage. There are many ways to get compounding benefits from the stock market without becoming investing experts. You could invest in the stock market through equity mutual funds or ETFs.

 **Term Explained**

ETF – Exchange Traded Fund – is a portfolio of securities that tracks a market index or the price of a commodity.

Once you have selected the ETFs or mutual funds (which is much easier to do than selecting stocks!), the fund manager manages the portfolio for you. The key is instilling the discipline and habit of investing in your child. Once you give them basic knowledge of the different ways to invest in the stock market, they can decide how to invest based on their interest.

 **Term Explained**

A Mutual Fund is a portfolio of stocks and/or bonds managed by expert fund managers.

The Investing Road Map

- Use games like Monopoly and the Game of Life to explain investing fundamentals.

- Open an investment account for them and invest regularly in shares or mutual funds. Show them the power of compounding at work.

- Let them invest in shares of companies they know. Let them do their own research. Review their portfolio with them on a weekly or monthly basis.

- When they turn 18, open an investment account and give them some money to learn investing.

- Once they understand the importance and fundamentals of investing, point them to resources to increase their knowledge.

Activities – With Younger Kids (ages 6–12)

Activity 1: Inflation

Inflation: What did these items cost when India became independent in 1947?[8]

1. Newspaper
    Answer – Re 0.13
2. Petrol (per litre)
    Answer – Re 0.27
3. Flight (Delhi to Mumbai)
    Answer – Rs 140
4. Cinema ticket
    Answer – Re 0.30
5. Milk
    Answer – Re 0.12
6. Raincoat
    Answer – Rs 4
7. 10 gm of gold
    Answer – Rs 88.62
8. Your grandfather's first salary
9. Monthly household expenses of your grandparents

Activity 2: Active versus passive income

There are two ways to make money and make your parents proud! One is to work for your money (active income – get a job or start a business). Another is to make your money work for you (passive income – invest in a business or stock market or an appreciating asset like land or gold). Choose the type of income – active or passive?

Krupesh's dad owns a flat in Khar and has rented it.
Answer – Passive income

Tia's dad has invested in shares of Colgate Palmolive and earns an annual dividend.
Answer – Passive income

Monica's dad is the CEO of a company.
Answer – Active income

Rohan's dad owns and runs a famous restaurant in Bandra West.
Answer – This one is more complex; his salary is active income, but the profits from the restaurant are passive income

Activity 3: Types of assets

Asset types (Appreciating versus Depreciating). Choose the right answer.

Appreciating assets over time
- Increase in value – *Answer*
- Decrease in value

Which of the two is an appreciating asset?
- Xbox
- Painting by M.F. Husain – *Answer*

Depreciating assets are purchased
- To use and enjoy – *Answer*
- To grow your money for the future

Which of the two is a depreciating asset?
- Home
- iPhone – *Answer*

Activity 4: Risk versus Return – Which investment is higher risk and may be higher return?

Case 1
- Investment A: You invested Rs 100 you will receive Rs 105 after 1 year.
- Investment B: You invested Rs 100 you will receive between Rs 90 and Rs 125 after 1 year. – *Answer*

Case 2
- Investment A: You invested Rs 100 you will receive between Rs 105 and Rs 110 after 1 year.
- Investment B: You invested Rs 100 you will receive between Rs 85 and Rs 135 after 1 year. – *Answer*

Case 3
- Investment A: You invested Rs 100 you will receive between Rs 95 and Rs 115 after 1 year.
- Investment B: You invested Rs 100 you will receive between Rs 50 and Rs 200 after 1 year. – *Answer*

Money Tasks for Teenagers

Investing milestone quiz

Use this quiz to gauge your teens' knowledge before you give them some money to invest.

1. Suppose you had Rs 100 in a savings account and the interest rate was 4 per cent per year. After 5 years, how much do you think you would have in the account if you left the money to grow?
   a. Exactly Rs 120
   b. Less than Rs 120
   c. More than Rs 120 – *Answer*

2. Imagine that the interest rate on your savings account was 4 per cent per year and inflation was 5 per cent per year. After 1 year, how much would you be able to buy with the money in this account?
   a. More than today
   b. Exactly the same
   c. Less than today – *Answer*

3. What is investing?
   a. Investing is very risky. Only people with a lot of knowledge about the markets should invest.
   b. Investing is a way to steadily grow your money, without taking much risk.
   c. Everyone should invest in appreciating assets like stocks, bonds, gold and real estate to grow their money to beat inflation. – *Answer*

4. If you buy a company's stock
   a. You own a part of the company. – *Answer*
   b. You have lent money to the company.
   c. You are liable for the company's debts.
   d. The company will return your original investment to you with interest.

5. If you want to get higher returns from your investments, you will have to invest in riskier investments.
   a. True – *Answer*
   b. False

6. Sarita owns shares of Reliance Industries. Her investment gives her dividends every year and the value of the shares has appreciated over time. She is guaranteed to receive dividends in the future and the value of her investment will keep increasing over time.
   a. True
   b. False – *Answer*

7. The difference between fixed deposit and stocks is
   a. Stocks are traded in the market, but fixed deposits are not.
   b. The value of stocks goes up and down every day. The value of fixed deposits does not fluctuate so much.
   c. Fixed deposits generally give lower returns compared to stocks over the long term.
   d. All of the above. – *Answer*

8. Investing in the stock market gives you guaranteed returns quickly.
   a. True
   b. False – *Answer*

9. If you start investing at a very young age, you will use time to compound your wealth.
   a. True – *Answer*
   b. False

10. The best way to invest in the stock market is
    a. To buy shares in a few good companies and hold them for long periods of time. – *Answer*
    b. To buy and sell stocks on a daily or weekly basis.
    c. None of the above.

Money Talks – Curated Financial FAQs for money conversations with your children

How can I double my money quickly?

There is no magic money potion. It's dependent on how much risk you are willing to take. If one is willing to take risks, the rewards (or losses) can be high and fast. If one doesn't want to take risks (fixed deposits or government bonds, for example), then the rewards are smaller, but steadier.

What are shares?

A share is a unit of ownership in a company. Owning shares

of a company makes you eligible to get a share of the profits, called dividends. You can buy and sell shares in a company with the help of a broker or through an online trading account.

Why do share prices go up and down every day?

Shares are traded in the stock market. Shares of companies do not have an MRP. Prices are based on the supply and demand for the shares on that day. For example, the demand for shares of companies that successfully created the coronavirus vaccine increased, increasing the price of the shares of these companies. Or when the government builds more roads, car sales increase, and share prices of auto companies increase.

What if the price of shares you own starts falling?

For example, I own one share worth Rs 100 of a company called Awesome. Let's assume Awesome was shut for a few months during the pandemic and the company made losses. No one likes a loss-making company, so people who owned Awesome shares started selling them and the price went down to Rs 90. Technically, the value of my share has gone down right now but I haven't made a loss (yet). If I sell my shares of Awesome at Rs 90, then I'll make a Rs 10 loss.

Sometimes shares of financially sound companies also fall for various reasons – the overall trend in the market, a bad quarter, raw material issue, or sluggish demand. But if the issues are resolved, the company will bounce back to the same or higher share price. So, if I liked Awesome, I didn't sell, waited for the lockdown to end, and then next year Awesome share price reached Rs 150. So now my share is worth Rs 150, or if I sell it, then I make a Rs 50 profit.

What is a bond?

When you invest in a bond, you lend money to the company (or the government, if it is a government bond). The company pays you interest every year and gives you your money (called face value) back after a fixed period of time.

What is a mutual fund?

A mutual fund is a portfolio of stocks and/or bonds managed by expert fund managers. These managers charge a fee to give you a return above the market average. You have to choose the mutual funds carefully because not all funds end up giving you above average returns.

What is an ETF?

An Exchange Traded Fund is a basket or portfolio of stocks or bonds that mimics the performance of the overall market or part of the market. For example, you can own an ETF that will give you the same returns as the Sensex or you could own an ETF that gives you the same performance as that of the IT or auto sector. ETFs can also track the price of a commodity, like gold. These funds charge very low fees because they only mimic the performance of all or part of the market.

What is the Sensex?

Sensex is a basket of 30 of the largest and the most actively traded stocks on the Bombay Stock Exchange. This basket reflects the overall performance of the stock market.

People say that you should invest in the market when it is low. How do you time the market?

With so many investors buying and selling shares for different reasons, it is next to impossible for even the savviest investors to predict if the markets will go up or down in the short term. Smart investing is not about timing the market, but about time in the market.

6

Conscious Borrowing

'Doesn't EMI stand for Easy Money Instalments?'
— Reyansh, age 15

> **Key Financial Habits**
> - Understand the cost and consequences of debt
> - Make a repayment plan
> - Create a backup plan

Does your child think that someone is rich because they have a fancy car and lots of branded goods? When your child thinks of net worth or wealth, they typically think of what they see – which are the assets. But net worth is what you OWN minus what you OWE.

Our children understand the concept of *owe*. At some point, they may have borrowed money for some reason or another – a forgotten wallet or less cash. As parents we always teach our children not to borrow, and if they've borrowed, to pay it back immediately. This is what we were taught and so we teach our children the same.

Fun Fact

Indian household debt has increased from 2.2 per cent of GDP in 2000 to 12.4 per cent of GDP in 2020.[1]

Yet, as incomes grow, the average Indian household is not only consuming more, but also borrowing more to fund their purchases. Oftentimes they do so only to keep up with neighbours and friends. Our teenagers are constantly bombarded with messages that promote consumerism. Will this influence them to make unsustainable financial choices? Many young adults often spend recklessly when they start earning. Thrilled at the thought of financial freedom, they purchase with EMI payments without fully understanding or planning for them.

 Term Explained

EMI: Equated Monthly Instalments is the amount you pay each month when repaying a loan. This includes the interest and principal.

Borrowing is not always a bad thing, but it has consequences. Our children must understand the responsibility and risks of taking on debt before they earn

 Research

49 per cent of new borrowers are below the age of 30.[2]

Conscious Borrowing

and manage their own money. This will help them avoid major financial pitfalls. This chapter focuses on how you can help your children understand the cost and consequences of borrowing.

What our children should know about borrowing

What is the cost of borrowing?

Debt costs money. When our children borrow from their friends they pay back the same amount. However, buying things on EMI costs more because you have to pay back the loan plus the interest and the loan fees (administrative cost associated with taking a loan).

What are the consequences of borrowing?

Debt hangs on long after the thrill of the purchase is gone. When we borrow we are stealing from the future to pay for today's purchases (or investments). And if we cannot repay the loan, due to job loss or a financial emergency, the interest continues to accrue, and the loan burden continues to rise. Missing EMI payments often results in a downward spiral,

>  **Term Explained**
>
> A credit score is a number between 300 and 900 that depicts a borrower's ability to pay back a loan. Anything above 700 is considered a good score. Lenders use this score to decide how much to lend to you.

decreasing our credit score, and affecting our future ability to borrow.

What to consider before borrowing?

Before our children borrow from a friend now or later as young adults from a bank, these are the three questions they should answer.

1. Do I absolutely want this now? Can I save up for it and get it later? Again it's about instant versus delayed gratification.
2. How will I repay the loan? What is my repayment plan?
3. How can I mitigate the risks associated with borrowing? What is my backup plan in case of job loss or an unforeseen emergency? (Ideally the backup should not be you, the parent!)

The COVID-19 pandemic brought to the fore all the worst-case scenarios we believed could never happen, from deaths to sudden loss of income. A parent talked to us about his experience of borrowing just around the pandemic. 'We borrowed heavily to set up a new restaurant in January 2020. And then the rest is history, but not in a good way. We planned for a slow start but not the worst-case scenario, a complete closure like this. If it weren't for our investment portfolio, we'd be on the streets. We hope it never happens again, but planning for a loan is definitely a lesson I'll be teaching my children,' explains Atul.

Is borrowing always bad?

Sometimes it makes sense to borrow. If your purchase is an investment that will grow over time, then borrowing may be a good idea. For example, if you know that the value of your house will increase over time, it may be wise to get a housing loan. Borrowing to buy a phone or a car or a TV may not make sense, because they are depreciating assets. (Remember, we talked about this in the previous chapter!) Why pay more (cost + interest) for an asset that will lose value?

Note: Sometimes a car manufacturer may give you a 0 per cent interest loan. If there are no hidden costs, this may be a good deal. Always check on the interest rate and fees before you borrow.

How to inculcate the right attitude towards borrowing in your children

Discuss your own loans, if any

If you have a home loan or a car loan, talk to them about how the loan works and how you have planned on paying back the loan. Talk to them about your backup plan, in case you lose your job or your business does not do well. There are many EMI calculators online that you can use to show them the cost of taking a loan.

Explain credit score

Show them your credit score. You can print a free report at https://www.cibil.com/freecibilscore. You can discuss how credit scores are calculated, what are the factors that affect credit scores and why it is important to maintain a good score.

Hands-on loan experience

Give your child some hands-on experience with borrowing, especially when they absolutely must have something. A father we spoke to, Vikas, said his son, Sahil, wanted fancy headphones. Vikas told him he would pay the amount upfront, but Sahil would have to give him Rs 500 per month for a year from his pocket money. 'I just wanted him to experience that sometimes the headphone thrill is short term but paying EMIs is a long-term thing. Sahil paid the instalments for 1 year, and still uses the headphones. He says he loves them, so I'm glad the thrill wasn't short term. But it's an important life lesson all kids should learn.'

Some parents want their kids to learn first-hand the responsibility of taking a loan. 'Kids must learn the discipline of paying back what they owe,' says Vinay, another parent we spoke to. Even though he could afford to pay for his child's education abroad, Vinay took an education loan. He wanted his son to work hard and value the education he would receive. We asked him about whether the loan was worth taking because of the high interest. He said it was a small cost to pay for an important lesson.

Practise with a credit card

When your children get older (18 years and above), you can get them a credit card with a low credit limit instead of a debit card. In general, it is much easier to overspend with credit cards, because you are not paying from a limited amount of cash in your wallet. Using a credit card at a younger age with parental supervision will help children build good credit habits. Show them how bills must be paid on time every month. You can also show them the consequences of being late on payment, i.e. the interest and other fees.

If you do not want to give your child a credit card, then show them how you pay your credit card bills. Show them a credit card statement; discuss the high interest rate and late fees most credit cards charge.

You should not borrow for depreciating assets. Does that mean we can never have good things in life?

Very often, people make a conscious choice to enjoy a better car or an expensive phone on EMIs and pay interest on a depreciating asset. This is a personal choice, based on one's risk appetite and earning potential and one that our children will also have to make for themselves as they grow up. Understanding the cost and consequences of taking on debt will help them make a well-informed decision.

Borrowing Road Map

- Talk to your children about the cost and consequences of borrowing money.
- Discuss your plan for paying back your home loan or car loan.
- Lend them money for something they want and let them pay for it over time with their pocket money.
- Show them your credit card statement and discuss the high cost of credit card debt.
- Give them a credit card when they are over 18 years and help them build good credit habits.

Activities

Activity 1: Good Debt versus Bad Debt

Review the short stories below and determine the impact these decisions will have on the character's financial future.

Story 1

Neena just moved into her rented apartment in a new city for her first job. She would like to buy the latest TV for her apartment. With rent and other expenses, there is not much left over to save from her salary. She decides to take advantage of a financing offer from a local electronics store and buys the TV on EMI.

Is this a good or bad debt decision? Why?

Story 2

Jyoti wants to buy her own home. She has enough money saved up to make the down payment. She is doing well at her job and hopes that she will continue to rise up the corporate ladder. She is thinking of taking a home loan.

Is this a good or bad debt decision? Why?

Story 3

Niraj has heard that opening a credit card account is a good way to build credit. Some months he charges a lot to the card and cannot pay his credit card bill in full. He only pays the minimum balance.

Is this a good or bad debt decision? Why?

Activity 2: Calculate the cost of debt

Calculate the interest in the different scenarios using any online EMI calculator.

Scenario 1

Ravi wanted to buy the iPad Air. It cost Rs 54,900. He did not have enough savings to pay for it, so he bought it on EMI – Rs 5,191 for 12 months. The interest rate is 24 per cent.

Calculate the cost of debt, i.e. the total interest payable.
– *Answer: Rs 7,395*

Scenario 2

Sona wanted to buy a Samsung 43-inch smart TV that cost Rs 36,999. She bought it on EMI – Rs 3,339 for 12 months. The interest rate is 14.99 per cent.

Calculate the cost of debt, i.e. the total interest payable.
– *Answer: Rs 3,072*

Money Talks – Curated Financial FAQs for money conversations with your children

How does borrowing affect my credit score?

A credit score is like your financial health report card. It helps banks decide whether to lend to you and how much interest to charge you (higher interest if your score is low). Being late on EMI payments or not paying the EMI for a few months impacts one's credit score negatively. On the flip side, if one does not borrow money, the person will not have a credit score and banks are unwilling to lend to someone with no credit score. The easiest and cheapest way to build a credit score is to get a credit card and pay the bills on time.

What is the difference between a debit card and a credit card?

A debit card and a credit card look the same, but when you pay for something with your debit card, the money is deducted instantly from your bank account. If you don't have enough money in the bank account, the debit card transaction will be declined. You can charge your purchase to a credit card, but you have to pay for these purchases at the end of the month.

Why can't I just charge my credit card when I don't have money to buy something?

You can keep charging your credit card up to a certain amount (the credit limit). But you will have to pay for these purchases at the end of the month when you receive the credit card bill. If you do not have enough money to pay the credit card bill then you will have to pay interest on the unpaid amount. Credit cards charge a very high interest rate, 25–30 per cent. Spend as much as you can pay back at the end of the month.

Expert Speak

How financial experts talk to their children about money

Nilesh Shah, Managing Director, Kotak Mahindra Asset Management. He has two daughters. One is studying medicine and the other works at the United Nations in Healthcare & Public Policy.

My wife and I have a modest lifestyle, so the kids never saw us being extravagant. They followed our example and are conscious of their spending. We always talked about our simple roots. I took my children to the chawl where I grew up and explained to them that I could only study because of scholarships.

From a young age, I took my girls to work every Saturday. I showed them the Bloomberg terminal, the trading room, my office space, etc. My colleagues enjoyed their visits and were happy to talk to them about their jobs and the markets. Discussions on the stock markets, companies and balance sheets were frequently part of our dinner table conversations.

The girls listened and asked many questions. They could always tell from my mood when I came home from work, whether the stock market had gone up or down that day. My daughters also observed and learned the importance of hard work when they saw the long hours I put in.

Parents usually teach their children to earn and save, but I would advise them to also show their kids how to keep and grow their money. Parents should give a small amount to their kids to invest on their own. That way they can commit small mistakes early on and avoid big blunders later in life. Parents can encourage their children by letting them keep the gains on their portfolio above a certain benchmark return. This will motivate them to invest and take appropriate risks. Although my daughters didn't join the investing industry, they understand the markets and economics and have learnt how to manage their money.

Giving has been an important part of our life. Both my wife and I volunteer. The kids observed and followed. They chose their own causes and we supported them.

Our parenting philosophy has always been, don't just say it, practise it because kids are observing. If you spend a lot, so will they. If you invest wisely, so will they.

7

Thanking Our Stars – Gratitude and Giving

'Thank you for showing me how to use the tongue cleaner.'
— Riya, age 5

> **Key Financial Habits**
>
> - Practise gratitude
> - Give regularly

A common concern among the parents we spoke to was entitlement. 'Our kids have everything they want. How do we prevent them from becoming spoiled and entitled?' says Tejal, a caring mother. It is easy for our kids to take their privilege for granted. Providing opportunities for gratitude and giving is a good way to insulate our children from the pitfalls of entitlement. As researcher Brene Brown said, 'What separates privilege from entitlement is gratitude.[1]

Fun Fact

Jamshedji Tata topped the list of the most generous philanthropists in the past 100 years. His total donations were valued at $102 billion. Bill and Melinda Gates were second at $74.6 billion.[2]

Practising gratitude

Research shows that grateful children and teenagers are happier, do better academically, help others and are less materialistic.[3]

How to help our children practise gratitude

Here are some examples of how different families practise gratitude.

Prayer

Some families pray together regularly. 'We do it for religious reasons, but I think saying grace is so important. It really makes our children take a minute to be thankful for the food on the table,' explains Andrea, a mother we spoke to.

Gratitude exercise

We often take our household help for granted. 'I always remind my children to thank them for the many little things that they do for us,' explains Rupal, a parent. Jyoti, an extracurricular activity teacher, asks all the kids to say one thing that they were thankful for at the end of every class. Another therapist we spoke to told us about a simple activity she does with her own children. At the end of a holiday or dinner at a special restaurant, she asks her children what they enjoyed most and what they were thankful for.

Thank you note

Thank you notes really force children to think about what they've really liked or appreciated and put those thoughts down on paper. (*Soneera's note:* At the end of every academic year, I ask my son to write a thank you note to his teachers. It really makes him think about the whole year and realise the effort that the teachers have put into his education. My sister does the same every time her children stay over with family friends.)

You can use any of these methods that work best for your household. But as always, consistency is key, so practise regularly. It will help your kids pause and think about what they have versus focusing on what they don't have.

Giving

Gratitude and giving are interrelated. Research shows that grateful people tend to give more.[4] Like gratitude, giving has many benefits. It increases physical and mental well-being, and it creates a happy high often referred to as 'helper's high' (and that's definitely the high we'd prefer to see our kids enjoying!). It also builds self-confidence when kids can see that their actions help make a difference.

How can we start our children along the giving journey

Many parents believe that giving/charity should come later in life, but we recommend starting at a very young age (above

6 years). The first step is talking to them about giving back and involving them in your charitable activities. Research shows that modelling charitable behaviour and talking to kids about giving helps them give more as adults.[5]

'During the first lockdown, my husband and I delivered groceries to our house help. My kids saw other families who were also in need. They asked us if we could help them too. We bought more grains and helped another ten families. They told their classmates, who did the same in their neighbourhood. We've made it a monthly thing now,' says Mamta, mom to 15-year-old Akash and 17-year-old Tanaya.

Mamta did not start the giving conversation with her children at age 6 or 7. She did it later, but managed to convey the message – that their family cares about their staff and their community and that it's important to help those in need.

Make them donate – money or in-kind

If you plan on giving them pocket money, give a little more so that they can set aside that money for giving (Rs 110 instead of Rs 100). If you do not plan on giving them pocket money then let them set aside a small amount of their gift money for giving. The amount is up to you, based on your financial situation and values.

When they are young you can help them donate that 'giving' money to a cause you like. When they are ready, they can choose a cause based on their interest. Being involved in the process will encourage them to give more.

Donations don't always have to be about money. (*Soneera's*

note: I personally think about all the times I saw my dad donate blood when I was a kid. He still regularly organises blood donation camps for our neighbourhood, and when I grew old enough, I started donating too. I still donate twice a year – it takes 15 minutes, it's free and it literally saves lives. And I'm hoping that when my children grow up, they will follow in my footsteps too.) Rajul, another parent we interviewed, gives on special occasions. 'On my daughter's birthday, we always send some cake and the birthday return gifts to the children of our house help. Also, on their birthdays we always give them a gift. My children enjoy the process of choosing their gifts,' she explains.

Encourage them to volunteer

Volunteering time and skills by engaging in a meaningful cause helps our children build self-confidence. 'Taking my child for the Juhu beach clean-up truly opened his eyes to a sense of community,' explains Shivani. 'He saw that he could make a difference. The beach was a cleaner place for him, and the plastic trash we collected helped save marine life. It drove home the concept of neighbourhood and how giving was not only about money, but about helping the world become a better place.'

When they are younger, they may not be able to volunteer with organisations. But they can certainly start helping close to home, maybe for neighbours or by doing something for the household help or their children. They can choose a volunteer organisation when they grow older.

Advocacy is another way of volunteering. During COVID-19, groups of people got together to provide services such as taxis to vaccination centres, lists of shops and hospitals stocking relevant medicines, hospital beds, and oxygen. Students and student groups amplified these organisations on social media to help their community.

My husband and I donate a lot but my child is not interested

This happens. Teenagers, especially, can sometimes be too wrapped up in their own world to grasp the significance of giving back. If your child is not interested in giving, do not force it. The point is to come from a place of understanding – not resentment.

Try to continue modelling the 'giving' behaviour. Try to have conversations around giving. When discussing current events like natural disasters or endemic problems like poverty, make the conversation positive and ask how we can help. Try and find a cause that aligns with your child's interest, such as drawing attention to the harmful effects of fast fashion or a local charity that encourages sport activities for children.

Gratitude and Giving Road Map

- Develop a regular practice of gratitude with your children.
- Start the giving conversation with your children as early as age 6.
- When they start getting pocket money or gift money, set aside some for 'giving'.
- Help them choose a cause that is meaningful for them.
- When the kids are young, let them help their neighbours, or your house help's family.
- As they grow older they can volunteer at an organisation.
- Encourage them to come up with ideas to help people in need. Support these ideas.

Activities for All Ages

At home

1. Take care of your neighbours' plants or pets when they are travelling.
2. Offer help to a sick neighbour or friend.
3. Spend some time with the elderly and help them feel less lonely (games work great!).
4. Consider supporting your staff – do they need help paying their kids' school fees? Do they need help before the rains to avoid water leakage in the house?
5. Write thank you notes to people who help or make a difference.

Volunteering

1. Help clean the beach or other common utility area.
2. Volunteer at a local NGO or a cause that needs help.
3. Collect newspapers, glass bottles and cans to recycle.
4. Help spread awareness about a cause or assist an NGO.
5. Start or sign petitions about a cause you believe in.

Donation

1. Give away leftovers or extra food to the needy.
2. Donate used clothes, books and other items.
3. Organise a bake sale or bazaar with friends to raise money for a cause.
4. Donate money from your allowance to a cause you believe in.

5. Organise drives (collecting supplies like pens and books) for less privileged kids.

Money Talks – Curated Financial FAQs for money conversations with your children

Should we give money to beggars?

Note to parents: A conversation that should be had, even if your child does not initiate it. Many families choose not to give money to beggars. Some do not want to encourage begging, some do not want the money to be used for purchasing alcohol or drugs, some do not want to help the gangs that exploit children and force them into begging. Some families prefer to give food. One parent we interviewed carried small packets of glucose biscuits in her purse to give beggars. Some families give money. Whether you give or don't give, the important part is talking to your child and explaining your reasons.

Why are we rich? Why is he poor?

Note to parents: This is a great opportunity to explain privilege to the kids. A large part of the opportunities available to us are because of where we are born – our school, our neighbourhood, our friends, our education, even job/business opportunities. Helping people who were not born into the same level of privilege is a good way to show our gratitude for winning the lottery of birth. You could also discuss ways in which the wealth gap can be reduced, which progresses into various topics such as economics, politics and even philosophy.

Why don't they print money and give to the poor?

We can print money and give it to the poor. But what will happen when it gets over? Do we print more? It's important to provide education and opportunity so that people can make money, especially the underprivileged. But we cannot print money and hand it out – for one, it will result in inflation (among many other issues), and two, we should encourage everyone to be a contributing member of society – if everyone gets money anyway, who would want to work?

8

To Be or Not To Be – Making a Career Choice

'Dad's work is so easy . . . he just sits on the computer all day.'

— Ansh, age 6, as his dad struggled to work from home during the pandemic

> **Key Financial Habits**
> - Explore careers
> - Develop a good work ethic
> - Explore entrepreneurship

The first step in wealth creation, whether you're a billionaire or an aspiring lakhpati, is working to earn money. Most of our children, like us, will spend a significant portion of their life working to sustain themselves, their families and their aspirations. We do not need research to tell us that parents have a huge influence on their children's career choices. However, as much as we'd like to, we also cannot dictate which careers our children choose.

Our job as parents is to try to give them access, education and exposure so they can make informed and balanced decisions. This chapter discusses different tools and knowledge we can give our children to help them find a career that is fulfilling, both financially and emotionally.

Why expose children to different career options early on

'When we graduated from school, our options were limited to arts, science and commerce. But things have changed now,' as college counsellor Nikita Mehta explains. 'Many children who come to us for counselling have vague ideas about studying business, but today business isn't the same as commerce. A business degree can mean a hundred things, from entrepreneurship, finance, marketing, HR, to sports management or even business communication.' With the number of options available to our children today, starting early will give them more time to discover their aptitude and interests. This is where our job as parents kicks in – by helping them explore opportunities in their area of interest or passion.

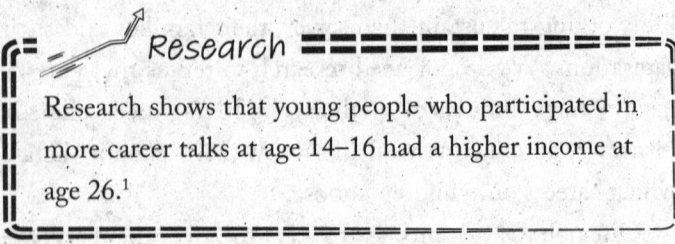

Research shows that young people who participated in more career talks at age 14–16 had a higher income at age 26.[1]

The career exploration process doesn't have to be tedious or stressful. In fact, it can be a fun and productive activity for the entire family. Some of the things to keep in mind as you help your children through this process of discovery:
- Spend time talking to them about your experiences.
- Listen to their hopes, dreams and fears.
- Be open to their ideas even if you may not agree with them.
- Get professional help if required.

How to help our children explore career options

Talk to them

When was the last time you discussed your day with your child, what you do at work or at home, and how you felt? If you're working on an interesting case (as a doctor or lawyer or project manager) tell your children what you're working on and what makes it interesting. If you're in the finance industry and the stock market has had a good run, let your children know you had a great day. Small conversations help children grasp the bigger picture!

(Soneera's note: One day, my son and I were watching TV and I said, 'You know, Megha masi works for the company that sponsors this show.' So he asked me, "What does Megha masi do?" I called her and she explained, in a very kid-friendly way, her role as the UI/UX lead and how she designs apps. After he hung up, he asked, "So what do Teertha masi, Niraali masi and Rowena masi do?" I told him, very briefly, what an orthodontist, owner of a design agency and a film producer/director do. He's only 7 but I wanted to encourage questions and talk to him about these things from an early age.')

Most parents enroll their kids in all kinds of extracurricular activities when they are young. When kids have 'phases' like taekwondo or quilling, they are learning about their aptitude, skills and interests as they join (and leave!) different classes. Do not focus on the results – 'did you come first?' or 'did you have the best poem?' Instead, focus on the process – 'what did you enjoy?' or 'what did you dislike?'

Take them to work or a meeting

'I love taking my kids to work with me. My younger one enjoys drawing on the drafting table, but the older one is 12 and he really understands when I show him different drawings and design choices,' explains Gaurang, an architect we interviewed.

Every career is associated with a different work environment. If you can, take your children to work a few times a year from a young age. At first, they will be amused by the smaller stuff such as stamps and ink pad, vending machines, and office stationery. As they grow older, they'll observe you and understand the finer details of your work. If taking them to work is not possible, take your kids to meetings. Most people don't mind if you bring your kids to a meeting, as long as they are not disruptive. Help your kids understand why you made the career choices you did – from your degree, to switching jobs, to the challenges you faced and the sacrifices you made.

A father we spoke to, Ram, a senior investment banker, brought his daughter to work every alternate Saturday so he could spend more time with her (and also to give his wife some much-needed time off). The father–daughter lunch on these Saturdays became a tradition for them. Ram reminisces, 'Neeya would ask a hundred questions – Why do I talk on the phone so much? Does mom also make money when she talks on the phone? and so on. At age 11–12, her questions were quite specific – How do I get clients? Why did that project get cancelled? Today, Neeya is 20 and studying law. She says those Saturdays were more valuable than some of her classes!'

Arrange internships and shadowing opportunities

Showing interest and aptitude in a subject is not enough to choose a career. Making a career choice is also about understanding the skills required, career progression possibilities, the work environment, the associated lifestyle, and day-to-day activities. When children get older (above 15 years), internships and shadowing (observing someone at work) are important steps in their career exploration journey. For example, Namita's son was good at maths and physics and also loved art. Architecture seemed like an ideal choice. When he interned at his father's friend's firm, he realised that designing was only one part of the job. It also involved project management and managing skilled and unskilled labour. He loved the design aspect but, in his words, 'I don't want to follow up with electricians and plumbers all day.' He is now exploring product design.

Internships and shadowing opportunities are difficult to arrange and may not be possible for many parents. But all of us have a network of friends and family who would happily talk to our kids and give them an opportunity to observe a day in their work life.

Use the internet

The internet has millions of videos and blogs that discuss careers in detail, and show you 'a day in the life of' a particular profession. Movies and books are also a great way to connect with your kids and discuss different careers (think *Wolf of Wall Street* or *Mary Kom* or *Dangal* or *The Pursuit of Happiness*). If they're interested in coding or technology, you can show them documentaries on Steve Jobs or Bill Gates, for example. As you discuss these, focus on the road to success more than the success itself.

Have focused discussions

As the kids grow older and the discussions about choosing a career become more serious, use the framework on the p. 151 to help your children make a decision.

When using their framework, some parents may advise their children to prioritise one of these aspects over the other. There is no right answer. At the end of the day, the child has to figure out a balance that works best for them (and it's quite reasonable that this balance may change over a period of time – one may choose money at 18 and happiness at 35).

Help them develop a good work ethic

Our child's attitude is also influenced by how we think of our jobs or profession. If children constantly hear a parent complain about their job, they will view working as a chore, something that pays the bills. If our child sees us excited about work, they will also be enthused about working.

Career Exploration Framework

- **Passion.** Your child's aptitude and interest. Many parents already know their child's aptitude and interests. You could make your child take a psychometric test to confirm what you may already know.

- **The realities of a job.** Discuss the lifestyle that comes with the career such as the work–life balance, the work environment, and the work hours.

- **Money.** Explore the monetary aspects of the career. Not just the starting salary, but the earning potential of the career in the long term.

Many children have also come to resent the 9-to-6 lifestyle, with memes all around about chasing happiness, not money. No job is happy every single minute. Any work, even if it's glamorous like being a supermodel or actor or influencer, or something more desk based like a chartered accountant, requires showing up every single day and doing your 'job'. Many kids think that posing for TikTok videos and creating content is fun and easy, but influencers will vouch for the hard work and discipline that goes behind the millions of views.

Fostering a sense of discipline and hard work goes beyond the checklist of values to give your child – these are the building blocks of your child's career and life.

Explore entrepreneurship

Entrepreneurship is something every parent should help their children explore. Many children have business ideas (creating a new app or starting a gourmet instant noodle menu, for example), that may (and probably will) fail. The lessons they learn about risk and reward will be invaluable to them as adults.

This pandemic has opened an array of entrepreneurial opportunities for parents and children. If your child sees you start a business, they'll view entrepreneurship more positively, as something that is achievable. 8-year-old Shiven learned how to make candles and sold them to friends and family for Rs 50 each to collect money for patients with COVID-19. Another budding entrepreneur, Athira, age 12, started her own babysitting services. She charged parents by the hour, and kept the kids at her house, while her parents or grandparents were home. She'd plan activities, games and snacks for the kids. All of these are small, but real examples of how entrepreneurship teaches children the importance of planning ahead, thinking about resources they'll need, executing their plans, and customer service!

My child wants to become a cricketer. He loves the sport, but I don't know if he is good enough to succeed and support himself financially

Certain professions involve high risk and high reward. Like acting, music and sports. If you succeed, you will do well financially, but the probability of success is very low. No parent wants to ask their children to give up their passion, but maybe a backup plan can help. Dhir wants to become a comedian, but his parents are acutely aware of the success rate and financial realities of the field. They discussed multiple options and Dhir has decided that he will continue to study for his accounting degree, alongside pursuing this career. If comedy doesn't work out in 2 to 3 years, he will look at master's programmes. Similarly, budding cricketers can discuss alternative career options to pursue if cricket doesn't work out.

Career Exploration Road Map

- Expose your kids to different careers early on.
- Talk to them about your job.
- Let them spend time with relatives and understand their work.
- Take your child to work or meetings.
- Arrange internships when they are older.
- Find a shadowing opportunity for them.
- Use YouTube and other internet resources to show them the realities of a career.
- Talk about hard work and dedication through movies and books.
- Give them opportunities to explore entrepreneurship.

Activity

Career exploration: Use this guide to compile your research on different careers

1. Brief description of career: List at least three responsibilities related to the career
2. Key requirements: Personality traits, skills.
3. Educational requirements: Degrees, certifications
4. Money prospects: Starting salary, future salary potential
5. Industry outlook: Growth prospect of jobs, risk of job loss
6. Career progression: Growth possibilities
7. Work environment: Work hours, shift work, travel involved, desk/out of office
8. Day in the life of: Tasks accomplished on a typical day
9. Positives: List at least three
10. Negatives: List at least three

Money Talks – Curated Financial FAQs for money conversations with your children

Are we rich? Or are we poor?

(*Note to parents:* As always, please try to understand why your child is asking you this question.)

We have more money than some people, but less money than some people. Comparing ourselves to others is not really helpful. We have enough to be comfortable and fulfil many of our needs and desires.

Why can't I go to study abroad like some of my friends?

Studying abroad is expensive. By the time a child is old enough to think about college applications (16–18 years), parents can sit down and explain gently that studying at a university in the US, for example, costs upwards of Rs 1 crore. Such a large amount may not be possible at this time; the focus should not be on the location of education but the quality of education. From IITs to Ashoka University to National Law School of India University, India now has many established new options for higher education.

(*Soneera's Note:* I know a parent who told his daughter that he could either afford a big wedding or a college education abroad. Similarly, parents have also offered their children seed money for a venture in lieu of a foreign education, and the children have been happier for that capital.)

Is someone with higher earnings or wealth more successful?

Depends on how you define success. Success is the accomplishment of an aim or purpose. For many, this aim or purpose is financial well-being. But for many it is about fighting for social injustice, saving the environment or caring for the sick.

Why do you work? Why don't you spend time with me?

I do spend time with you, but I also have to spend time working because I love what I do and I enjoy it, and this is important to me.

OR

Mom and dad make money when they work and this pays for all our necessities, comforts and luxuries.

OR

I'm sorry if you feel like I don't spend time with you. I have to work right now, but let's decide on a time that you and I can spend together later today or tomorrow and that will be our special time.

Why can't you earn more like my friend's dad?

Some jobs pay more and some pay less. I made the decision to do what I do based on my passion, my education and the lifestyle I want.

OR

Why do you ask? What do you like about your friend's or your friend's dad's life? There will always be people who are more successful than you, richer than you, have bigger houses or people who travel more than you. Our happiness or self-worth cannot be pinned to another's life.

Is education necessary for earning money? What about Dhirubhai Ambani or Sachin Tendulkar?

I agree with you. Education is not necessary to earn money. But education gives you access to opportunities that you may not otherwise have. For every Dhirubhai Ambani or Sachin Tendulkar there are a thousand failed entrepreneurs/

sportspersons who took other jobs when their dreams failed. Also, there is a difference between education and learning. Whereas Dhirubhai or Sachin may not have got an education, they did not stop learning and becoming masters in their own field.

But what if the career I love does not earn enough money?

We'd like you to pick a career that has a healthy mix of passion and financial stability. But if you want to follow a career that is fulfilling emotionally and not financially, you will have to be even more financially savvy and prudent than your peers with better earnings. You must learn to invest early, with any amount possible, spend judiciously and budget.

Building Good Financial Habits – Action Plan

Healthy financial habits are integral to raising a financially grounded child. In every chapter, we have included tools to help you inculcate these habits. We encourage you to make your own action plan using the table below. We wish you and your child(ren) luck on your money journey.

Financial Habits

Save Regularly
- Delay gratification
- Pay yourself first
- Plan for the future/Set goals
- Plan for emergencies

Action Plan

Mindful Spending
- Align with your values
- Practise self-control/Avoid impulsive buying
- Say 'no' to peer pressure
- Shop for value

Action Plan

Live Within Your Means
- Plan a budget
- Differentiate between wants and needs
- Track expenses

Action Plan

Keep and Grow Wealth
- Understand investing basics
- Invest and review regularly
- Increase investing knowledge

Action Plan

Give
- Practise gratitude
- Give regularly

Action Plan

Conscious Borrowing
- Understand cost and consequences
- Plan repayment
- Create a backup plan

Action Plan

Plan Your Future Career Path
- Explore career options
- Develop a good work ethic
- Explore entrepreneurship

Parting Thoughts

The Balancing Act

As you go through the money journey with your child(ren), we wanted to leave you with some final thoughts.

A holistic approach

One of the most common questions we were asked during our parent interviews was 'How do we teach our children about money, while making sure that they do not become money-minded?' As our children learn to make spending/saving/investing/giving decisions, we should help them understand that these decisions are not only related to money, but also to our overall values and priorities. For example, cutting back on eating out is not just about spending less and saving more, but also about eating healthy. Going out for an expensive dinner with friends occasionally is also about spending time with friends. A review of our credit card statement is not just about our expenses, but also about what we value – maybe clothes rank higher than eating out or books higher than clothes. A more holistic approach to our money conversations will help our children become mindful of money and its role in our lives, without becoming money obsessed.

Note: Review your credit card statement or overall household budget for a month or two. What are your most frequent transactions? This exercise in spending self-awareness will help you understand what you value and what your kids are learning from you.

Nurture counts, but so does nature

Two children in the same household, raised with the same values, can have completely opposite personalities. We've all experienced this at some point. Perhaps you have two kids where one child is a saver and the other is a spender. One is interested in investing, while the other in giving. As you create your action plan for inculcating good financial habits in your children, stress on balance – between saving and spending, enjoying our privilege and being thankful, and giving and investing. This will help your 'spender' child learn to save and the 'saver' child learn to spend and enjoy things once in a while.

The drops that build an ocean

James Clear, the author of *Atomic Habits*, said: 'Success is a product of daily habits – not once-in-a-lifetime transformations.' None of us have earned, saved or invested all our money at once. Small deposits and small investments have created the portfolio we have today. Many debt stories are also the result of a series of smaller bad decisions. As you continue on the money journey with your child, we encourage you to review your action plan regularly. Remember, it's the small habits practised regularly that will be the building blocks of a healthy piggy bank and eventually a successful portfolio.

Notes

1. Why Talk to Kids About Money

1. Dr David Whitebread and Dr Sue Bingham, 'Habit Formation and Learning in Young Children,' University of Cambridge/ The Money Advice Service, 2013.
2. Tom Popomaronis, 'Warren Buffett: This is the No. 1 Mistake Parents Make when Teaching Kids about Money,' CNBC Make It,' July 30, 2019.
3. Daniel Kahneman and Angus Deaton, 'High Income Improves Evaluation of Life but not Emotional Well-being,' Proceedings of the National Academy of Sciences 107, no 38 (September 2010): 16489–16493.

2. Pocket Money or Not

1. Whitebread and Bingham, 'Habit Formation and Learning in Young Children', University of Cambridge/The Money Advice Service, 2013.
2. A. Bucciol and M. Veronesi, 'Teaching Children to Save and Lifetime Saving: What Is the Best Strategy?' *Journal of Economic Psychology*, 45 (2014): 1–17.
3. Terrie E. Moffitt, Richie Poulton and Avshalom Caspi, 'Lifelong Impact of Self-control, Childhood Self-discipline

Predicts Adult Quality of Life,' *American Scientist* 101, No. 5 (Sept–Oct 2013): 352.
4. Amit Bapna, 'Five Things the New Generation Study by Turner International Has Revealed,' *Economic Times*, May 18, 2016.
5. Bucciol and Veronesi, 'Teaching Children to Save and Lifetime Saving: What Is the Best Strategy?' *Journal of Economic Psychology*, 45 (2014): 1–17.
6. Scott Rick, 'Tightwads and Spendthrifts: An Interdisciplinary Review,' Wiley Online Library, September 19, 2018.
7. Maria Gabriella Ceravolo, Fabri Mara, Fattobene Lucrezia, Polonara Gabriele and Raggetti GianMario, 'Cash, Card or Smartphone: The Neural Correlates of Payment Methods,' *Frontiers in Neuroscience*, November 05, 2019.

3. Of Piggy and Other Banks

1. Abheek Singhi and Kanika Sanghi, 'How India Spends, Shops and Saves in the New Reality?' BCG Report, 21 December 2020.
2. J. Ashby, I. Schoon and P. Webley, 'Save Now, Save Later? Linkages Between Saving Behaviour in Adolescence and Adulthood,' *European Psychologist* 16, no. 3: 227–37.
3. Goodreads, Quote by Brian Tracy, https://www.goodreads.com/quotes/943953-goals-are-the-fuel-in-the-furnace-of-achievement-the.
4. CNBC Make It, 'Kevin O'Leary Explains Compound Interest with a Piggy Bank,' YouTube Video, 1.25, May 31, 2018.
5. Victor Labate, 'Banking in the Roman World,' *World History Encyclopaedia*, November 17, 2016.

4. Shopping Trips and More!

1. Shristi02, '20 Interesting Facts About Indian Currency,' May 21, 2020, https://icytales.com/interesting-facts-about-indian-currency/.
2. Melbourne Child Psychology and School Psychology Services, 'Why Parents Should Feel Good about Saying "NO" to Their Children,' https://www.melbournechildpsychology.com.au/blog/why-parents-should-feel-good-about-saying-no-to-their-children/.
3. Dan Mager, 'Why Sometimes Saying "No" to Your Kids Is So Important,' Mager, Dan. 'Why Sometimes Saying "No" to Your Kids is So Important.' Psychology Today. January 20, 2019.
4. Sarah Berger, 'Tech-free Dinners and No Smartphones Past 10 pm – How Steve Jobs, Bill Gates and Mark Cuban Limited Their Kids' Screen Time,' CNBC Make it, June 05, 2018.

5. Grow Your Own Money Tree!

1. Erika Rawes, '5 Crazy Facts About Money That You May Not Know,' *USA Today*, July 26, 2014.
2. Goodreads, Quote by Warren Buffett, https://www.goodreads.com/quotes/8760232-if-you-don-t-find-a-way-to-make-money-while.
3. Shlomo Benartzi, 'If You Don't Save Enough, Perhaps You Have "Exponential Growth Bias",' *The Wall Street Journal*, June 16, 2019.
4. Bitcoin USD (BTC-USD), https://finance.yahoo.com/quote/BTC-USD/history/
5. Nithin Kamath, 'What does it take to win at trading?',

Z-Connect, June 26, 2020.
6. Motilal Oswal Group Site, 5 Key Quotes by Charlie Munger on Value Investing and Creating Wealth, https://www.motilaloswalmf.com/knowledge-centre/5-keys-of-investing/5-key-quotes-by-charlie-munger-on-value-investing-and-creating-wealth/69
7. Peter Lynch and John Rothchild, *One Up On Wall Street: How to Use What You Already Know to Make Money in the Market* (Simon & Schuster, 2000).
8. Sachin P. Mampatta, 'How Time Flies: In 1947, a Ticket from Delhi to Mumbai Cost More Than a Gold Coin,' *Mint*, August 16, 2017.

6. Conscious Borrowing

1. See https://www.ceicdata.com.
2. TransUnion Cibil and Google, 'Credit Distributed: A Thought Paper on Emerging Themes in the Consumer Credit Space,' June 10, 2021.

7. Thanking our Stars – Gratitude and Giving

1. Brené Brown's Quote Sourced From https://www.goodreads.com/quotes/858472-what-separates-privilege-from-entitlement-is-gratitude.
2. Chiranjivi Chakraborty, 'Not the Gates, Jamsetji Tata Is Philanthropist of the Century with $102 Bn in Donations,' *The Economic Times*, June 23, 2021.
3. Lan Nguyen Chaplin, Deborah Roedder John, Aric Rindfleisch and Jeffrey J. Froh, 'The Impact of Gratitude on Adolescent Materialism and Generosity,' *The Journal of Positive Psychology*, August 01, 2018.

4. C.M. Karns, W.E. Moore III and U. Mayr, 'The Cultivation of Pure Altruism via Gratitude: A Functional MRI Study of Change with Gratitude Practice,' *Front. Hum. Neurosci.* 11 (2017):599.
5. M. Ottoni-Wilhelm, D.B. Estell and N.H. Perdue, 'Role-modeling and Conversations About Giving in the Socialization of Adolescent Charitable Giving and Volunteering,' *J Adolesc.* 37, 1 (January 2013): 53-66.

8. *To Be or Not To Be – Making a Career Choice*

1. Elnaz T. Kashefpakdel and Christian Percy, 'Career Education That Works: An Economic Analysis Using the British Cohort Study,' *Journal of Education and Work* (April 27, 2016).

Select Bibliography

Ashby, J., I. Schoon, and P. Webley. 'Save Now, Save Later? Linkages Between Saving Behaviour in Adolescence and Adulthood.' *European Psychologist* 16, no. 3: 227–37. https://doi.org/10.1027/1016-9040/a000067

Bapna, Amit. 'Five Things the New Generation Study by Turner International Has Revealed.' *Economic Times*, May 18, 2016. https://economictimes.indiatimes.com/five-things-the-new-generation-study-by-turner-international-has-revealed/articleshow/52306526.cms.

Benartzi, Shlomo. 'If You Don't Save Enough, Perhaps You Have "Exponential Growth Bias".' *The Wall Street Journal*, June 16, 2019. https://www.wsj.com/articles/if-you-dont-save-enough-perhaps-you-have-exponential-growth-bias-11560737101.

Berger, Sarah. 'Tech-free Dinners and No Smartphones Past 10 pm – how Steve Jobs, Bill Gates and Mark Cuban limited their kids' screen time.' CNBC Make it, June 05, 2018. https://www.cnbc.com/2018/06/05/how-bill-gates-mark-cuban-and-others-limit-their-kids-tech-use.html.

Bitcoin USD (BTC-USD). https://finance.yahoo.com/quote/BTC-USD/history/.

Bono, Giacomo and Jeffrey Froh. 'Seven Ways to Foster Gratitude in Kids.' Greater Good Magazine, March 5, 2014. https://greatergood.berkeley.edu/article/item/seven_ways_to_foster_gratitude_in_kids.

Brown, Brené. What Separates Privilege from Entitlement Is Gratitude. Quoted in https://www.goodreads.com/quotes/858472-what-separates-privilege-from-entitlement-is-gratitude.

Bucciol, A. and M. Veronesi. 'Teaching Children to Save and Lifetime Saving: What is the Best Strategy?' *Journal of Economic Psychology*, 45 (2014): 1–17. http://dse.univr.it/home/workingpapers/wp2013n10.pdf.

Ceravolo, Maria Gabriella, Mara Fabri, Lucrezia Fattobene, Polonara Gabriele, and Raggetti GianMario. 'Cash, Card or Smartphone: The Neural Correlates of Payment Methods.' *Frontiers in Neuroscience*, November 05, 2019. DOI: 10.3389/fnins.2019.01188.

Chakraborty, Chiranjivi. 'Not the Gates, Jamsetji Tata is Philanthropist of the Century with $102 Bn in Donations.' *The Economic Times*, June 23, 2021. https://economictimes.indiatimes.com/markets/stocks/news/not-the-gates-jamsetji-tata-is-philanthropist-of-the-century-with-102-bn-in-donations/articleshow/83774898.cms.

Chaplin, Lan Nguyen, Deborah Roedder John, Aric Rindfleisch, and Jeffrey J. Froh. 'The Impact of Gratitude on Adolescent Materialism and Generosity.' *The Journal of Positive Psychology*, August 01, 2018. https://doi.org/10.1080/17439760.2018.1497688.

CNBC Make It. 'Kevin O'Leary Explains Compound Interest with A Piggy Bank.' YouTube Video, 1.25, May 31, 2018. https://www.youtube.com/watch?v=XjTQW4efqQc.

Global economic data, indicators, charts and forecasts. https://www.ceicdata.com.

Goodreads. Quote by Brian Tracy. https://www.goodreads.com/quotes/943953-goals-are-the-fuel-in-the-furnace-of-achievement-the.

Goodreads. Quote by Warren Buffett. https://www.goodreads.com/quotes/8760232-if-you-don-t-find-a-way-to-make-money-while.

Kahneman, Daniel and Angus Deaton. 'High Income Improves Evaluation of Life but not Emotional Well-being'. Proceedings of the National Academy of Sciences 107, no 38 (September 2010): 16489–16493. https://www.princeton.edu/~deaton/downloads/deaton_kahneman_high_income_improves_evaluation_August2010.pdf.

Karns, C.M., W.E. Moore III, and U. Mayr. 'The Cultivation of Pure Altruism via Gratitude: A Functional MRI Study of Change with Gratitude Practice.' *Front. Hum. Neurosci.* 11 (2017):599. https://doi.org/10.3389/fnhum.2017.00599.

Kashefpakdel, Elnaz T. and Christian Percy. 'Career Education That Works: An Economic Analysis Using the British Cohort Study.' *Journal of Education and Work* (April 27, 2016). DOI: 10.1080/13639080.2016.1177636.

Labate, Victor. 'Banking in the Roman World.' *World History Encyclopaedia*, November 17, 2016. https://www.worldhistory.org/article/974/banking-in-the-roman-world/.

Lynch, Peter, and John Rothchild. *One Up On Wall Street: How to Use What You Already Know to Make Money in the Market.* Simon & Schuster, 2000.

Mager, Dan. 'Why Sometimes Saying "No" to Your Kids is So Important.' Psychology Today. January 20, 2019. https://

www.psychologytoday.com/us/blog/some-assembly-required/201901/why-sometimes-saying-no-your-kids-is-so-important.

Mampatta, Sachin P. 'How Time Flies: In 1947, a Ticket from Delhi to Mumbai Cost More Than a Gold Coin.' *Mint*, August 16, 2017: https://www.livemint.com/Politics/CaDCEetFtAuoI63z06x2qJ/How-time-flies-In-1947-a-ticket-from-Delhi-to-Mumbai-cost.html.

Melbourne Child Psychology and School Psychology Services. 'Why Parents Should Feel Good About Saying "NO" to Their Children.' https://www.melbournechildpsychology.com.au/blog/why-parents-should-feel-good-about-saying-no-to-their-children/.

Moffitt, Terrie E., Richie Poulton, and Avshalom Caspi. 'Lifelong Impact of Self-Control, Childhood Self-discipline Predicts Adult Quality of Life.' *American Scientist* 101, No. 5 (Sept–Oct 2013): 352. https://www.americanscientist.org/article/lifelong-impact-of-early-self-control.

Motilal Oswal Group Site. '5 Key Quotes by Charlie Munger on Value Investing and Creating Wealth.' https://www.motilaloswalmf.com/knowledge-centre/5-keys-of-investing/5-key-quotes-by-charlie-munger-on-value-investing-and-creating-wealth/69.

Ottoni-Wilhelm, M., D.B. Estell, and N.H. Perdue. 'Role-modeling and Conversations About Giving in the Socialization of Adolescent Charitable Giving and Volunteering.' *J Adolesc*. 37, 1 (January 2013): 53-66. doi: 10.1016/j.adolescence.2013.10.010. Epub 2013 Nov 20. PMID: 24331305.

Popomaronis, Tom. 'Warren Buffett: This is the No. 1 Mistake

Parents Make when Teaching Kids about Money.' CNBC Make It, July 30, 2019. https://www.cnbc.com/2019/07/30/warren-buffett-this-is-the-no-1-mistake-parents-make-when-teaching-kids-about-money.html.

Rawes, Erika. '5 crazy facts about money that you may not know.' *USA Today*, July 26, 2014. https://www.usatoday.com/story/money/business/2014/07/26/crazy-money-facts/13107853/.

Rick, Scott. 'Tightwads and Spendthrifts: An Interdisciplinary Review.' Wiley Online Library, September 19, 2018. https://doi.org/10.1002/cfp2.1010.

Shristi02, '20 Interesting facts About Indian Currency,' May 21, 2020, https://icytales.com/interesting-facts-about-indian-currency/.

Singhi, Abheek and Kanika Sanghi. 'How India Spends Shops and Saves in the New Reality?' BCG Report, December 21, 2020. https://www.bcg.com/en-in/how-india-spends-shops-and-saved-in-the-new-reality.

TransUnion Cibil and Google. 'Credit Distributed: A Thought Paper on Emerging Themes in the Consumer Credit Space.' June 10, 2021. https://www.transunioncibil.com/resources/tucibil/doc/insights/reports/transunion-google-credit-distributed-report.pdf.

Whitebread, Dr David and Dr Sue Bingham. 'Habit Formation and Learning in Young Children'. University of Cambridge/The Money Advice Service, 2013. http://mascdn.azureedge.net/cms/the-money-advice-service-habit-formation-and-learning-in-young-children-may2013.pdf.

Kamath, Nithin. 'What does it take to win at trading?' Z-Connect, June 26, 2020. https://zerodha.com/z-connect/traders-zone/tradingpsychology/what-does-it-take-to-win-when-trading.

Acknowledgements

Writing is a solo journey but publishing most definitely is not.

We are extremely grateful to Zarin Daruwala, Nilesh Shah and Anup Maheshwari for taking the time out to talk to us and giving us valuable parenting and money insights. Thanks to Alaokika Motwane, Desire Dias and Dr Shweta Avarsekar for being so generous with their time and advice. A very special thanks to Rakesh Jhunjhunwala, Raamdeo Agarwal, Deepak Parekh, Vijay Shekhar Sharma, Nikhil Kamath and Kunal Bahl for giving us such encouraging feedback. We are eternally grateful to the many parents who agreed to in-depth interviews and shared their financial and parenting stories so openly.

We'd like to thank our editor Chiki Sarkar, who placed faith in our first draft. It's been a pleasure to work with you and the entire team at Juggernaut, especially Jaishree Ram Mohan, Biji Lalachan, M.R. Maithreyi and Haitenlo Semy.

We will always be grateful to publishing veteran, Ashok Advani, for his continued support and encouragement. Our heartfelt thanks to Aditi and Mehul, for being there from start to finish.

Acknowledgements

Binal's note:

I have spent countless hours with thousands of school and college students through our financial education program, Finance GYM. Most students focus on acquiring the education needed to earn money but don't know that it is equally important to learn the skills to manage and grow the money you earn. In general, young people who recognize the importance of money management come from families that encourage the development of these skills from an early age. The seeds of financial education are sown at home, over dinner table conversations, shopping trips and vacations. I hope this book encourages parents to spend more time helping their children build a strong foundation in money management.

I want to thank Soneera for being a fun and easy companion through this writing journey. I am extremely grateful to my friends, Mila and Prashant Desai, Monita Jhaveri, Rupali Shah and Priyanka Bhartia, for devoting many many hours to reading and discussing the book. A special thanks to my friend, Meghana Bheda from Creative Autumn for creating simple and beautiful graphics, for the book. The book literally would not look the same without you. I will always be indebted to my friend and author, Payal Kapadia, for giving me great insights into the publishing world. She was the first one to read the book and encourage me to publish it. Thanks to my niece, Dhruvi, for sharing her ideas on how we could reach out to more parents through this book. Most of all, I could not have written this book without the love and support of my parents, Saroj and Madhukant – I love you Forever & Always, my husband, Parth – the King of My Heart and my daughters, Riya and Mira – my Love Story(s). I am the Lucky One.

Soneera's note:

When I had my first child, I felt what most parents feel – that I want to provide my child the best of everything. But there's a fine line between giving our children the world and raising entitled children. The more I researched and the more experts we spoke to, two things became abundantly clear – (1) our children will mirror our behaviour, not our advice and (2) the importance of starting these conversations with children from a young age. Through this book, we have tried very hard to make financial literacy fun and accessible. I hope that it encourages all parents to raise a generation of financially grounded boys and girls (especially girls).

Thank you Binal for a stress-free writing process and for being so easy-going. My most heartfelt gratitude goes to Shefali Nath Gupta for helping us with the survey and being such a great sounding board. Our research would not be the same without you. My time under Parthasarathi Swamy has significantly influenced how I outline and write and I'm grateful for the time I worked with him. Thank you Deeksha Khanna and Richa Vohra for listening and all the feedback. To Megha Agarwal, Teertha Karnakar, Niraali Parekh and

Acknowledgements

Rowena Baweja for your love and friendship. This book would not have been possible if my mother-in-law had not watched my kids while I wrote and edited. Thank you Bharti and Kirit Mehta for your encouragement and love. Thank you Nupur and Rima for the sister (in-law) hood. To Viral and Megan, for all the love. To my parents, Nita (you are my rock) and Jayant Sanghvi, you two are my world. To Nikita for loving me like a daughter and Minita who thought I wrote well even when I didn't and to whom I owe much in life. To Ansh and Annika, if there was a baby lottery, I've defied the odds and won it twice. And lastly to Yash, thank you for loving me the way you do. You are my sthanabalam.

A Note on the Authors

Binal Gandhi is CEO of The Learning Curve Academy and the founder of the gamified financial education program, Finance GYM (Grow Your Money). Through this program, she has engaged with over 20,000 youth and conducted over 100,000 hours of teaching at various corporates, colleges and schools across India. Finance GYM has been offered at top colleges like SP Jain Institute of Management and Research, NMIMS, Welingkar Institute of Management, Tata Institute of Social Sciences and corporates like IIFL, Tata Communications and Julius Baer. Finance GYM has been covered in publications like *Economic Times*, *DNA*, *The Hindu* and *Business India*.

Binal has worked for close to 20 years in the areas of Corporate Finance and Mergers and Acquisitions. Before starting The Learning Curve Academy, Binal was Managing Director at Navigator Capital Advisor and Executive Director at MAPE Advisory Group, consulting companies on cross-border acquisitions and fund raise. Prior to that, as Senior Vice President in charge of Mergers and Acquisitions at Wells Fargo in the US, Binal led teams that resulted in acquisitions worth over $1 billion. She started her career at GE Capital in the US, where she was a Six Sigma Black Belt. Binal has taught courses in Corporate Finance and Mergers and Acquisitions at NMIMS and is currently visiting faculty at SP Jain, where she teaches a course in Wealth Management. Binal has an MBA and a master's degree in Electrical Engineering from Purdue University. She has two daughters aged 13 and 18, who have been a strong source of inspiration for her work in financial education.

∽

Soneera Sanghvi worked as a lawyer in New York before moving to India and becoming Assistant Editor at *Business India*. She has an undergraduate degree in Finance (BMS) from NM College and a Juris Doctor from University of Arizona. Soneera is also the co-founder of an education consultancy, High Skies Co, which helps students craft stand-out college application essays. Over the last decade, Soneera has written for a wide range of clientele, including several leading multinational companies. She is also mom to two toddlers, aged 3 and 7, and her daughter inspired her on the journey to this book when she said 'You save, I'll spend'.

juggernaut

THE APP FOR INDIAN READERS

Fresh, original books tailored for mobile and for India. Starting at ₹10.

juggernaut.in

CRAFTED FOR MOBILE READING

Thought you would never read a book on mobile? Let us prove you wrong.

juggernaut.in

Beautiful Typography

The quality of print transferred
to your mobile. Forget ugly PDFs.

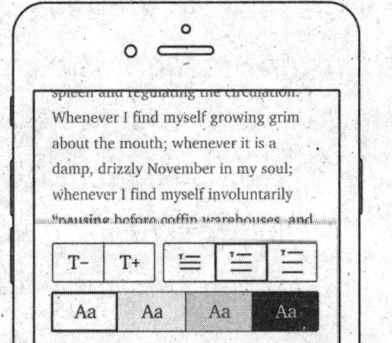

Customizable Reading

Read in the font size, spacing
and background of your liking.

juggernaut.in

AN EXTENSIVE LIBRARY

Including fresh, new, original Juggernaut books from the likes of Sunny Leone, Praveen Swami, Husain Haqqani, Umera Ahmed, Rujuta Diwekar and lots more. Plus, books from partner publishers and loads of free classics. Whichever genre you like, there's a book waiting for you.

juggernaut.in

3

DON'T JUST READ; INTERACT

We're changing the reading experience from passive to active.

juggernaut.in

A Note on the Authors

Ask authors questions

Get all your answers from the horse's mouth. Juggernaut authors actually reply to every question they can.

Rate and review

Let everyone know of your favourite reads or critique the finer points of a book – you will be heard in a community of like-minded readers.

Gift books to friends

For a book-lover, there's no nicer gift than a book personally picked. You can even do it anonymously if you like.

Enjoy new book formats

Discover serials released in parts over time, picture books including comics, and story-bundles at discounted rates. And coming soon, audiobooks.

juggernaut.in

4

LOWEST PRICES & ONE-TAP BUYING

Books start at ₹10 with regular discounts and free previews.

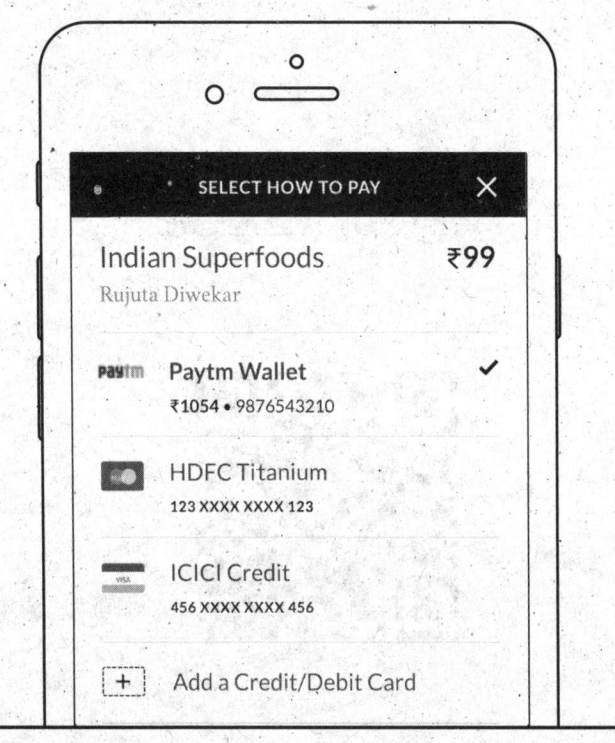

Paytm Wallet, Cards & Apple Payments

On Android, just add a Paytm Wallet once and buy any book with one tap. On iOS, pay with one tap with your iTunes-linked debit/credit card.

To download the app scan the QR Code
with a QR scanner app

For our complete catalogue, visit www.juggernaut.in
To submit your book, send a synopsis and two
sample chapters to books@juggernaut.in
For all other queries, write to contact@juggernaut.in